LEGO® MINDSTORMS® NXT-G Programming Guide

James Floyd Kelly

LEGO® MINDSTORMS® NXT-G Programming Guide

Copyright © 2007 by James Floyd Kelly

ISBN-13 (pbk): 978-1-59059-871-9

ISBN-10 (pbk): 1-59059-871-7

eISBN-13: 978-1-4302-0303-2

Printed and bound in the United States of America 9 8 7 6 5 4 3

Lead Editors: Jim Sumser/Jonathan Hassell
Technical Reviewer: Fay Rhodes
Editorial Board: Steve Anglin, Ewan Buckingham, Gary Cornell, Jonathan Gennick, Jason Gilmore, Jonathan Hassell, Chris Mills, Matthew Moodie, Jeffrey Pepper, Ben Renow-Clarke, Dominic Shakeshaft, Matt Wade, Tom Welsh
Project Manager: Richard Dal Porto
Copy Edit Manager: Nicole Flores
Copy Editor: Heather Lang
Assistant Production Director: Kari Brooks-Copony
Senior Production Editor: Laura Cheu
Compositor: Ellie Fountain
Proofreader: April Eddy
Indexer: Broccoli Information Management
Artist: Kinetic Publishing Services, LLC
Cover Designer: Kurt Krames
Manufacturing Director: Tom Debolski

Distributed to the book trade worldwide by Springer-Verlag New York, Inc., 233 Spring Street, 6th Floor, New York, NY 10013. Phone 1-800-SPRINGER, fax 201-348-4505, e-mail orders-ny@springer-sbm.com, or visit http://www.springeronline.com.

For information on translations, please contact Apress directly at 2855 Telegraph Avenue, Suite 600, Berkeley, CA 94705. Phone 510-549-5930, fax 510-549-5939, e-mail info@apress.com, or visit http://www.apress.com.

The source code for this book is available to readers at http://www.apress.com in the Source Code/ Download section.

For Dan, Belle, Sarah, and Jake—my "Texas family"

Contents at a Glance

About the Author xi
About the Technical Reviewer. xiii
Acknowledgments. xv
Introduction xvii

CHAPTER 1   Robots and Programs 1
CHAPTER 2   Program Structure 7
CHAPTER 3   Hello World! 11
CHAPTER 4   Get Movin'. 21
CHAPTER 5   Record and Play Back. 29
CHAPTER 6   Make Some Noise! 33
CHAPTER 7   Wired!. 39
CHAPTER 8   True or False?. 47
CHAPTER 9   Feedback 53
CHAPTER 10 Wait for It!. 63
CHAPTER 11 Round and Round 71
CHAPTER 12 Decisions, Decisions. 83
CHAPTER 13 Stop It. 95
CHAPTER 14 Pick a Card, Any Card 99
CHAPTER 15 Apples and Oranges 105
CHAPTER 16 Inside or Out? 115
CHAPTER 17 Yes? No? Maybe? 125
CHAPTER 18 Title = Anything You Like 133
CHAPTER 19 Basic Text. 147
CHAPTER 20 Basic Math 151
CHAPTER 21 Staying Alive. 155

CHAPTER 22   Your Own Filing Cabinet 157

CHAPTER 23   Calibration 163

CHAPTER 24   Get Reset 167

CHAPTER 25   Messages 171

CHAPTER 26   My Block Is Your Block 177

APPENDIX   Math Basics for NXT 185

INDEX 189

Contents

About the Author xi
About the Technical Reviewer xiii
Acknowledgments xv
Introduction xvii

▩CHAPTER 1	**Robots and Programs**	1
	What Is a Robot?	1
	What Is a Program?	1
	NXT-G	4
▩CHAPTER 2	**Program Structure**	7
	What Do I Mean by Structure?	7
▩CHAPTER 3	**Hello World!**	11
	The DISPLAY Block	11
	Data Hubs	16
▩CHAPTER 4	**Get Movin'**	21
	The MOVE block	21
	Moving Forward and Backward	22
	Stopping	24
	Steering	24
	Power Settings	25
	Duration Settings	25
	Braking and Coasting	27
▩CHAPTER 5	**Record and Play Back**	29

■CHAPTER 6   **Make Some Noise!** 33

The SOUND Block 33
    Action Settings 34
    Note Settings 34
    Control Settings. 35
    Function Settings 35
    Volume Settings 35
    Wait Settings. 35

■CHAPTER 7   **Wired!** 39

Passing Around Information 39

■CHAPTER 8   **True or False?** 47

One or the Other 47

■CHAPTER 9   **Feedback** 53

What's Your Condition? 53
Configuring the Sensors 54
    NXT Touch Sensor. 55
    RIS Touch Sensor 56
    NXT Sound Sensor 57
    NXT Light Sensor. 57
    RIS Light Sensor 58
    NXT Ultrasonic Sensor. 58
    NXT Rotation Sensor 59
    RIS Rotation Sensor. 59
    RIS Temperature Sensor 60
Other Input Types 60
Using the Blocks 61

CHAPTER 10 Wait for It! 63

The WAIT Block 63
    The LIGHT SENSOR WAIT Block 66
    The NXT BUTTONS WAIT Block 66
    The ROTATION SENSOR WAIT Block 67
    The SOUND SENSOR WAIT Block 67
    The TIMER WAIT Block 68
    The TOUCH SENSOR WAIT Block 69
    The ULTRASONIC SENSOR WAIT Block 69

CHAPTER 11 Round and Round 71

Do It Again and Again and Again... 71
Nested Loops 78

CHAPTER 12 Decisions, Decisions 83

Left or Right? Door 1 or Door 2? 83

CHAPTER 13 Stop It 95

The STOP Block 95

CHAPTER 14 Pick a Card, Any Card 99

The RANDOM Block 99
The NUMBER TO TEXT Block 101

CHAPTER 15 Apples and Oranges 105

The COMPARE Block 105

CHAPTER 16 Inside or Out? 115

The RANGE Block 115

CHAPTER 17 Yes? No? Maybe? 125

The LOGIC Block 125

■CHAPTER 18   **Title = Anything You Like** 133

The VARIABLE Block 133

■CHAPTER 19   **Basic Text** 147

The TEXT Block 147

■CHAPTER 20   **Basic Math** 151

The MATH Block 151

■CHAPTER 21   **Staying Alive** 155

The KEEP ALIVE Block 155

■CHAPTER 22   **Your Own Filing Cabinet** 157

The FILE ACCESS Block 157

■CHAPTER 23   **Calibration** 163

The CALIBRATE Block 163

■CHAPTER 24   **Get Reset** 167

The RESET MOTOR Block 167

■CHAPTER 25   **Messages** 171

The SEND MESSAGE Block 171

■CHAPTER 26   **My Block Is Your Block** 177

Creating a My Block 177

■APPENDIX   **Math Basics for NXT** 185

Converting Between Degrees and Rotations................... 185
Converting Degrees and Rotations into Distances 186
The X/Y Coordinate System in NXT 188

■INDEX 189

About the Author

JAMES (JIM) FLOYD KELLY is a freelance technical writer and currently lives in Atlanta, Georgia. With degrees in English and Industrial Engineering, his friends and family often wondered what he was thinking about when he made that decision. Well, he somehow managed to turn his skills into a career where he gets to play with robots, new software, and other technologies. Jim was one of the original Mindstorms Developer Program (MDP) participants selected by LEGO to test the new Mindstorms NXT robotics kit, and he contributes, with other NXT experts, to The NXT Step Blog (`http://www.thenxtstep.com`). He is also a member of the Mindstorms Community Partners (MCP), a group of NXT testers that continues to work with LEGO on the NXT product line.

About the Technical Reviewer

■FAY RHODES is a freelance graphic designer with a love of learning. She's become a great fan of LEGO Mindstorms NXT and is currently the only member of The NXT Step Blog who is a woman. Fay has gifts for building things and problem solving, which are put to good use designing creative, noncompetitive NXT robots.

Acknowledgments

I always read the acknowledgments page when I buy a new book. I like to know a little more about who helped shape a book and how it came to be, so I hope you'll take a second and read a little about the excellent team I got to work with to make the book that you're holding a reality.

A huge *thank you* goes to the team at Apress. You can read a complete list of the names of the persons involved in this book a few pages back, but just know that everyone at Apress has worked hard to bring this book to completion. I do need to point out the three individuals that I was most involved with during the editing of this book—Richard Dal Porto, Laura Cheu, and Heather Lang. The book is much improved as a result of their hard work.

Technical books need another pair of eyes to check and double-check that errors are eliminated. For that job, I get to thank my technical editor, Fay Rhodes (and her husband, Rick). I've worked with Fay and Rick on The NXT Step Blog for some time now, and it was nice to have them checking my work. This book is better because of their due diligence.

And finally, I have to acknowledge my fellow contributors at The NXT Step Blog for their ideas, questions, concerns, comments, and general sharing of information. Many times I approached them with questions of my own and got straight and accurate answers. For everything from screenshots to the CAD building instructions to great programming examples, I must thank them all.

Introduction

So, you want to learn to write really great programs for your Mindstorms NXT robots, huh? I totally understand. You can build the most awesome robot you and your friends have ever seen, but if all it does is spin around or count from one to three, no one is going to be impressed. What you want is to match the amazing construction of your bot with an amazing program, right? Absolutely! You wouldn't be reading this book if you weren't interested in improving your programming skills.

Let me first tell you that I'm not a programming guru. I've had many computer programming classes in my past, but I don't do this for a living. What I do is enjoy building and programming my own little collection of bots, just figuring out things as I go. I will be the first to admit that many of the programs I write are ugly (meaning they are sometimes quickly thrown together without any planning involved). But some programs I write are extremely elegant (the opposite of ugly—they're well planned, developed, and tested). But whether the program is ugly or elegant, it usually works. It works, because I spend the necessary time figuring out how to use the tools that are provided with the NXT programming language.

And that's the key point I want you to take from this Introduction: *The more familiar you are with the tools available to you in the programming language, the more easily you'll be able to write some powerful programs for your robots.*

Finally, if you've got any questions or comments about the book, feel free to e-mail me. My e-mail address is jktechwriter@gmail.com, and I'd love to hear from you.

James Floyd Kelly
Atlanta, GA
June 2007

■ ■ ■

CHAPTER 1

Robots and Programs

If you are already familiar with the subject of robots and the concept of programming, feel free to skip ahead a few chapters. But if you are just starting out with your LEGO Mindstorms NXT robotics kit and are asking yourself questions such as, "How is a robot different from a toaster?" or "Just what is this thing called programming?" then you're in the right place. If terms like "conditional statements," "nested loops," and "variables" make your head spin, don't worry—they make my head spin, too.

There is simply no reason that learning to use the Mindstorms NXT robotics kit should cause stress. It's supposed to be fun, right? Building robots and making them do what you want them to do shouldn't cause headaches. I don't like headaches, and I certainly don't want to give you one, so sit back and let me show you a less stressful method for getting the most out of NXT.

What Is a Robot?

I'm going to keep this short—I promise. What is a robot? There are numerous definitions. One definition is a human-shaped mechanical device that mimics human actions. Another definition is an electronic machine that functions independently, without human control. And there are many more. There truly doesn't seem to be one official definition.

For the purpose of this book, I'm going to give you my definition. Here goes: *A robot is a device that is built to independently perform actions and interact with its surroundings.*

In a nutshell, a robot should be able to move and react all on its own. If you are controlling its actions, it's just a remote-controlled toy, right? But if your device can do things like examine its surroundings, respond to obstacles such as chairs or walls, pick out a red ball from a mix of colored balls, and hundreds of other activities without help from its human creator, then you've got a robot.

You can build a robot using all the great Mindstorms NXT components that came with your robotics kit. Your bot can have claws or hands. It can have ears to listen and eyes to see. It can walk on legs or roll on wheels. But in order for a robot to be able to do all these things on its own, you must provide it with one additional component, a program.

What Is a Program?

I know I told you that computer terminology makes my head spin, but there are some terms that cannot be avoided. But the terms I want to introduce to you are easy to explain and even easier to spell, so they can't be all that bad!

When we talk about the Mindstorms NXT robotics kit, we're talking about a piece of technology. Technology almost always requires a little learning, but that shouldn't mean it has to be boring—NXT robots are cool and fun. So, let's start right off by defining one of the coolest technical terms you need to understand—*program*.

I can't really write a book about NXT programming without defining what a program is, can I? So let's jump in with a small discussion about this word. I promise to keep it fun.

Let's take a look at a very basic robot. I call this robot SPOT and, for right now, SPOT only does one thing. He sits.

Take a look at Figure 1-1; there's SPOT doing what he does best.

Figure 1-1. *My bot SPOT*

Can we all agree that SPOT is a fairly boring robot? We all know that robots should do things! You could almost say that SPOT needs to be trained. And that's how I'm going to define the word "program." Read the next two sentences slowly: A *program* is a set of instructions for my robot. *Programming* is what you do when you create a program.

It's not a long definition, and it certainly isn't complicated. The definition will get a little more detailed as you read more chapters, but for now, let's just start out with that very basic idea.

You've encountered a lot of programs in your lifetime. Don't believe me? Okay, let me give you an example:

Teacher: Okay, class, take out your history books.

[*Grumbling, the students take out their books.*]

Teacher: I want everyone to turn to page 55.

[*With more grumbling, everyone turns to page 55.*]

Teacher: Everyone read through to page 65.

[*Loud grumbling*]

The teacher just gave a program to follow: take out your book, turn to a specific page, and read a specified number of pages. Let me give you one more example:

Step 1: Place the widget firmly against the whatsit.

Step 2: Snap the special wonder-whatchamacallit into the widget.

Step 3: Flip the whatsit over, and bend the thingamajig to the left.

Those are steps I found in an instruction manual—a program for me to follow. If I follow the steps, my whatsit should work perfectly (my whatchamacallit still isn't working!).

A simple program is just a set of instructions (written, spoken, or maybe provided in some other method) that needs to be followed. I certainly don't want to call you a robot, but in a way, we all can frequently act like robots. When we follow a set of instructions, we are running a program! (Another word you might sometimes hear used instead of "run" is "execute": "I told SPOT to *run* his SLEEP program" is the same as "I told SPOT to *execute* his SLEEP program.")

Let's go back to SPOT. He's just sitting there. How boring. Let's pretend for a moment that SPOT has ears, and I can give him some instructions. I'll start off by giving SPOT some basic movements:

Me: SPOT, move forward.

[*SPOT starts to roll forward.*]

Me: SPOT, stop.

[*SPOT stops rolling.*]

I've just given SPOT two very simple programs to follow. What? Two programs? Yes, the first program is "Move forward." The second program is "Stop." The simplest programs can be just one step! Now, I could combine them into one program, but I'll encounter a problem:

Me: SPOT, move forward and stop.

[*SPOT just sits there.*]

What happened? Well, think about someone telling you to "move forward and stop." How far forward will you move? When will you stop? You're smart, but robots are not. Robots must be told *exactly* what to do. And in this example, SPOT did exactly as he was told. SPOT moved forward and stopped. The reason you didn't see him move is because the moment he started spinning his motors, he stopped.

In the first example, I waited until SPOT began to roll before telling him to stop, so he had time to actually move. In the second example, I combined the instructions into one program (move forward and stop) without telling SPOT how far or maybe how long (in time) to move forward. So let's try it again:

Me: SPOT, move forward for 5 seconds and stop.

[*SPOT moves forward for 5 seconds and then stops.*]

Okay, so maybe SPOT isn't the problem. I've just figured out that when I tell SPOT to do things, I've got to be *very* specific.

One other thing that SPOT is good at is reading my handwriting. Let me give you another example of how specific I need to be when telling SPOT to execute a program, but this time, instead of telling him what to do, I simply take out a piece of paper and write down the following: SPOT, move forward 3 inches; turn left 90 degrees; move backward 2 inches; spin 360 degrees, and stop.

Next, I give the piece of paper to SPOT, and he reads it. He moves forward 3 inches, turns left 90 degrees, moves backward 2 inches, spins 360 degrees, and, finally, stops.

If your NXT robot is like mine, though, it probably doesn't have the ability to listen to voice commands or read a sheet of paper.

If your robot can't hear you or read your handwriting, how exactly do you tell it what to do? Easy! You're going to use programming software. There are other names such as programming suite or graphical programming environment, or blah blah blah—for now, let's just use programming software, OK?

You're in luck—your Mindstorms NXT robotics kit comes with programming software called NXT-G (the *G* is for "Graphical," meaning programs are not written instructions such as my previous handwritten steps for SPOT).

■Note There are a lot of ways to program. Just as different people speak different languages, robots (and computers and other technical stuff) can speak different languages. Some examples of human languages are English, Spanish, French, German, and Italian. For your NXT robots, there are a variety of languages, too. I speak English, because that is the language I learned to speak in school. Your NXT Brick comes from the factory understanding one language: NXT-G.

I also speak Spanish. But it's not my native language. Your NXT Brick can learn to speak other languages, too, but its native language is NXT-G. Most people won't learn another language until they understand their native language well. And that's what you need to do—learn NXT-G well so you can talk to your robot (by giving it a program).

NXT-G

NXT-G is the tool you will use to tell your robots what to do. NXT-G allows you to create programs that can be *uploaded* (installed) to your NXT robot. These programs can be instructions as simple as "move forward 2 inches and stop" or as advanced as you can imagine! NXT robots can be built with a variety of motors and sensors. But without a good program, your robot won't know what to do: Do I spin my motors? What do I do with this Touch sensor? Without programming, you'll have one confused robot on your hands.

NXT-G is installed on a computer (there are Windows and Macintosh versions) and exists as software. I'm not going to be covering the basics of using the software, so you'll need to refer to the *LEGO Mindstorms NXT User Guide* that came with your NXT kit for installation instructions and steps on how to perform basic steps such as creating new programs, saving programs, and other items.

You will create and save your programs (just like you save a drawing or an essay on your computer) and then connect your NXT robot to the computer. When your NXT robot is connected, you will be able to upload one or more programs to your robot and run (execute) them.

Right now, there are two versions of the Mindstorms NXT-G programming tool. One version comes with the NXT robotics kit that's bought in a store (sometimes called the retail version), and the other comes with NXT kits bought through the LEGO Education division (sometimes called the education version). Education versions are typically purchased by schools and teachers, but anyone can actually buy this version if they wish.

If you're not sure which version you have, take a look at Figures 1-2 and 1-3. Figure 1-2 shows the retail version (with the Robo Center), and Figure 1-3 shows the education version (with Robo Educator). Don't stress too much over the version you own; there are differences, but for the purposes of this book, over 90 percent of the tools are identical.

Figure 1-2. *NXT-G retail version comes with Robo Center*

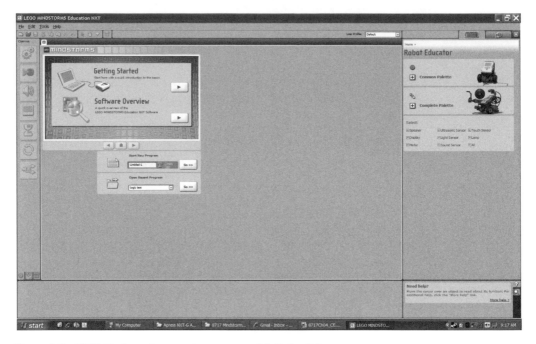

Figure 1-3. *NXT-G education version comes with Robo Educator*

The NXT-G Programming Software is fun to use; feel free play around with it. The best part about NXT-G is that much of it is extremely easy to figure out on your own. When you're ready to start learning how to create some awesome programs, turn to Chapter 2. I'm keeping the chapters short so you'll have plenty of time to read a little and then go play—no 50-page chapters in this book!

The next chapter is going to help you figure out what you want your robot to do. Go and experiment a little with NXT-G, and I'll see you in Chapter 2.

CHAPTER 2

■■■

Program Structure

I don't really like using technical terms like "program structure," but it is a very useful concept that will benefit you as you begin to program your robots. So bear with me for this short chapter.

What Do I Mean by Structure?

Back in Chapter 1, I gave you some examples of real-world programs. Would the following example have made any sense?

> **Teacher:** Class, open your books to page 55.
>
> [*The class looks confused.*]
>
> **Teacher:** Class, I want you to get out your history books.
>
> [*Giving the teacher confused looks, the students get out their books.*]

How can you read page 55 if you haven't yet been told which book to open? You might answer, "Yes, but I'm in history class, and the teacher said turn to page 55. So I'm sure the teacher means my history book!"

That's true. As a human, you are able to figure out certain instructions on your own. But remember—robots aren't that smart! They need to be given very strict and specific instructions. And those instructions need to be given in a specific order. That order is another way of saying "program structure."

Let's get out SPOT for another example. He's still doing his one and only trick—sit. We're not quite ready to upload an NXT-G program yet, but let's do some preplanning at this stage. I want you to use something that computer programmers call *pseudo-code*. What is pseudo-code? Well, the definition of "pseudo" is fake (as in pretend, simulated, virtual—get the idea?); it's not real. And "code" is simply another word for program. So put it all together and one way of looking at pseudo-code is this: fake program.

Our fake program isn't going to be written using NXT-G. The best way I can tell you to start creating a fake program is to pretend that SPOT has ears and tell SPOT what you want him to do. Let's try writing some pseudo-code using a numbered list:

1. SPOT, move forward until your Touch sensor is pressed and released; then stop.

2. Okay, SPOT, I want you to turn left 90 degrees.

3. Good job, SPOT. Now move backward until your Light sensor detects something black; then stop.

4. Now, SPOT, do a little dance.

That's pseudo-code? Well, it's a form of pseudo-code. Remember how I told you there are different programming languages? People write pseudo-code differently, too. The point I want you to understand is that before you can really program your robot using NXT-G, you need to have an idea of exactly what your robot will be doing. And the easiest way to do this is to simply write down, in simple language, instructions for your robot. That's the beginning of a good structure for the future NXT-G program.

When you write pseudo-code, you are accomplishing two things:

- You are gaining a better understanding of the tasks your robot will perform.

- You are creating an ordered set of instructions (structure) for your robot to follow.

You will use this pseudo-code to assist you when you begin to create your program with NXT-G. One final thing I want to mention about pseudo-code is that each instruction you give the robot should be as simple as possible. Take a look at the next two examples and tell me which one has the simpler instructions:

- *Example 1*: SPOT, move forward about 10 inches; turn left 90 degrees, and start moving forward; then start looking for a black object with your Ultrasonic sensor, because I want you to stop when you find a black object; then turn right 90 degrees, and move backward 2 feet, OK?

- *Example 2*:

  - SPOT, move forward 10 inches and stop.

  - Now turn left 90 degrees.

  - Starting moving forward, and turn on your Ultrasonic sensor.

  - Stop when you find a black object.

  - Turn right 90 degrees and stop.

  - Now move backwards 2 feet and stop.

Which example is less complicated to read? If you said Example 2, you are right. Let's be honest—some humans would be confused if you gave them the instructions in Example 1! When writing pseudo-code, break down your instructions into short and simple statements for your robot. This will make it easier for you to convert your pseudo-code to an NXT-G program.

Are you wondering how you convert pseudo-code to a real NXT-G program? Let me give you a small preview of what's to come in the chapters ahead.

Take a look back at my original pseudo-code for SPOT and read step 3, "Now move backward until your Light sensor detects something black; then stop."

If I am programming in NXT-G and am familiar with all the tools it contains, I would realize that there are tools (called *blocks*) that match up to my pseudo-code. Let me explain briefly.

When I want SPOT to move backward, he's going to use his motors, right? Well, I'll be using something called a MOVE block. The MOVE block will allow me to program my bot to spin the motors (and wheels) in reverse, so SPOT moves backward.

I only want SPOT to back up until his Light sensor detects the color black. To do this, I'll use something called a SENSOR block to monitor the Light sensor. The SENSOR block will be programmed to look for the color black.

Finally, I want SPOT to stop when the SENSOR block detects the color black. For this, I can use another MOVE block that tells the motors to stop spinning.

You will use these blocks and many more to properly program your robot to follow your instructions. This book will teach you about all the different NXT-G blocks, so you'll know which ones to use when converting your pseudo-code to an NXT-G program.

Okay, I told you this chapter wouldn't be long, and I meant it. If you can remember one thing from this chapter, it should be this: Programming your robot will be much easier if you take the time to write down the pseudo-code. If it helps, pretend your robot has ears, and tell it what you want it to do. Write down these instructions, and keep them short and simple.

In the next chapter, we're going to actually write some pseudo-code and convert it to an NXT-G program. The key to writing excellent NXT-G programs is understanding how the NXT-G programming blocks work; when you know how the blocks work, you'll know which blocks to use when converting your pseudo-code.

Chapter 3 is going to demonstrate the DISPLAY block, a very useful block that gives your robot the ability to write things to its LCD screen for others to read.

CHAPTER 3

■ ■ ■

Hello World!

There is a tradition in the world of programming for the first program you write to display the words "Hello World!" on the screen. In keeping with tradition, I'm going to show you how to create a simple version of this program for SPOT. This will allow me to demonstrate one of the simplest blocks included with the NXT software—the DISPLAY block. Once we've taken care of tradition, I'll show you the rest of the DISPLAY block's features.

The DISPLAY Block

In Chapter 2, I explained to you the concept of pseudo-code. Let me now give some pseudo-code to SPOT: SPOT, I'd like you to display the words "Hello World!" on your LCD screen.

Pseudo-code doesn't get much simpler than this. All I want SPOT to do for now is put the words "Hello World!" on his LCD screen. To convert this pseudo-code to an NXT-G program, I'm going to use the DISPLAY block.

Let's start by opening up the NXT software and entering **HelloWorld** in the Start New Program text box (see Figure 3-1). Click the Go button, and the HelloWorld program is open and ready.

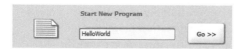

Figure 3-1. *Start a new program called HelloWorld*

Figure 3-2 shows the new program opened (see the tab called HelloWorld in the upper left corner?) and ready for you to start dropping NXT-G blocks. The word "Start" appears on the work space beam, telling you where your first programming block will be placed.

Figure 3-2. *The HelloWorld program is open and ready for the DISPLAY block.*

Are you ready for this? I want you to click the DISPLAY block on the Common Palette and hold down the mouse button. Drag and drop the block on the beam where it says "Start" (see Figure 3-3).

Figure 3-3. *The DISPLAY block*

Anytime you drop a block on the work space, the block's configuration panel will be displayed in the lower left corner of the screen. The configuration panel is where you will be doing most of the programming work for your bots. The configuration panel is similar to a car's dashboard. In a car, you can tune to a specific radio station, turn on the windshield wipers, and even find out the car's speed from the speedometer. The configuration panel allows you to turn on and off certain things as well as receive feedback. For example, you can use the DISPLAY block's configuration panel to choose what to put on the LCD screen, but the DISPLAY block can also receive input from items outside your control, just like your car can display a warning light on the dashboard when you need to check the oil or fill up on gasoline. Figure 3-4 shows the configuration panel for the DISPLAY block you just dropped on to the work space. To see the configuration panel for a block, simply click the block using the Pointer tool, and an aqua-colored band will appear around the block that is selected.

■**Note** If you select multiple blocks, no configuration panel will be displayed.

Figure 3-4. *Configuration panel for the DISPLAY block*

Now, to have SPOT's LCD screen display the words "Hello World!", make sure you've first selected the DISPLAY block (click it with the Pointer tool).

As you can see in Figure 3-4, by default, the DISPLAY block's Action section has a drop-down menu with the Image option selected (there are four options: Image, Text, Drawing, or Reset). Click the drop-down menu, and select Text from the options listed. You will now see a text box with the words "Mindstorms NXT" inside. Change the text to **Hello World!**, and you'll see the same text displayed in the Position section's preview box on the right side of the configuration panel (see Figure 3-5).

Figure 3-5. *The "Hello World!" text is displayed in the preview box.*

Now, using the File menu, select Save, and use the Browse button to choose a location to save the file on your computer. Click the Save button when you are finished. After saving, connect SPOT to your computer, and upload the HelloWorld program.

■**Note** For the remaining chapters in the book, you'll need to remember to save your programs. I won't keep bugging you with instructions to save your programs and upload them to your robots. OK? Just get in a habit of saving often.

After the program is uploaded, select it from the File section, and press the orange button on the Brick to run the program.

Did you see it? The program probably ran so quickly that you didn't even see the text displayed! Why does this happen? Well, when the program runs it is supposed to write "Hello World!" to the LCD screen and then end. And that's exactly what happened—the text displays, and the program ends. This happens *so fast* that you don't even get to see the text displayed. The good news is that this is very easy to fix, so let me update my pseudo-code before I continue: SPOT, I'd like you to display the words "Hello World" on your LCD screen for 10 seconds.

There are numerous ways to keep the text on the screen until you have a chance to read it, but I'm only going to show you one method in this chapter. You'll discover other methods as you continue with the book.

To fix this problem, I'd like you to move the mouse pointer over the WAIT block icon on the Common Palette. When you do this, a collection of WAIT blocks will appear on a fly-out menu, as shown in Figure 3-6.

Figure 3-6. *Adding a WAIT block will allow you to view the "Hello World!" text.*

The WAIT block does exactly what it says—it waits. As you can see in Figure 3-6, there are many different types of WAIT blocks, but the one I'm interested in right now is the WAIT block that allows me to specify how many seconds to wait. That would be the TIME WAIT block (the block that is circled on the fly-out menu in Figure 3-6).

Select the icon for the TIME WAIT block, and place it immediately after the DISPLAY block. In the configuration panel for the TIME WAIT block, select a reasonable time for the text to be displayed—my pseudo-code asked SPOT to wait for 10 seconds, so that is what I will configure (see Figure 3-7).

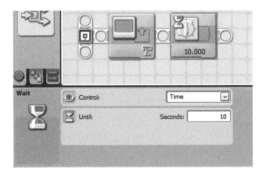

Figure 3-7. *Configure the TIME WAIT block for 10 seconds.*

Now run the program. You should see the text "Hello World!" display on the LCD screen for 10 seconds before the program ends.

You're probably thinking what I'm thinking, "That wasn't that exciting." But remember this: with programming, you have to start somewhere. And, in a few simple steps, you've now figured out how to add text to the LCD screen for any robot you build in the future. Now, let's look at some of the other things you can do with the DISPLAY block.

■**Note** Every program block has its own unique settings, so each configuration panel is different. Sections for the DISPLAY block, for example, include Action, Display, File, Text, Type, and Position. Sometimes, a section will not be visible until other options are selected. Don't let this worry you; I'll be going over all the unique items for each block throughout the book.

Here are details for the DISPLAY block's sections:

The Display section only has one configurable item—a Clear checkbox. When this box is checked (and the block is executed in a program), the Brick's LCD screen will be cleared of any text or images that are currently on the screen. After the screen is cleared, the DISPLAY block will put what you configured on the screen.

If you leave the box unchecked, any text or graphics you configure the DISPLAY block to put on the LCD will display on the screen along with whatever is currently displayed, instead of replacing it.

This is useful when you want text to appear on multiple lines; you can use multiple DISPLAY blocks to keep adding text to make sentences and even paragraphs. And, without clearing the screen, you can create your own simple images using the Drawing option in the Action section, which I'll explain next.

With the Action section, you have four options in the drop-down menu: Image, Text, Drawing, and Reset. By default, the drop-down menu is set to Image for a new DISPLAY block placed on the work space.

When you select Image in the drop-down menu, the File section is displayed; this section gives you access to a collection of small built-in pictures that can be displayed on the LCD screen (see Figure 3-8).

Figure 3-8. *Choose an image from the File section to place on the LCD.*

By clicking and holding the image in the preview pane on the right side of the configuration panel, you can drag the image around the small pane and place it wherever you wish. You can also use the X and Y coordinates to type in numbers that will place the image at a location of your choosing (see this book's appendix for a brief explanation of the X/Y coordinate system if you're unfamiliar with it). You can use this ability to move the image around the preview pane to place multiple images (which require using additional DISPLAY blocks) on the LCD screen.

The next option in the Action drop-down menu is Text. You've already used this in the previous "Hello World!" example, but I'd like to add that you also have the ability to drag the text around the preview pane and place it in a particular location. The LCD screen is broken into eight horizontal lines; you can use the small drop-down box next to the Preview pane to choose a number between 1 and 8 to define the line where text is placed.

The third option in the Action drop-down menu is Drawing (see Figure 3-9). You can choose to draw a line or a circle or to place a single point on the LCD screen, so your artistic talents will be somewhat limited. To create a detailed drawing, you would have to place dozens or more DISPLAY blocks one after the other, and the combination of lines, circles, and points would create the image. But the Drawing options can be useful to draw boxes around other text on the screen, so keep that in mind.

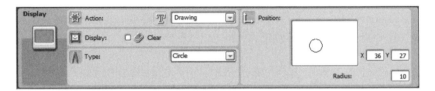

Figure 3-9. *The Drawing option can be used to place points, lines, and circles.*

To use the Drawing tool, select Point, Line, or Circle from the Type section (this section only appears if you have selected Drawing in the Action drop-down menu). For the point, you can drag it around the Preview pane and place it anywhere. You can also use the X and Y coordinates to place the point more accurately.

If you choose the Line, the end point of the Line is at position 10,10 (in the lower left corner). Click anywhere in the Preview pane to draw a line from that point to the place where you clicked. You can change the end point (10,10) by entering new coordinates in the X and Y boxes. You can also type in X and Y coordinates for the other end of the line for more accurate control over it.

Finally, for the circle, you have the option of changing the radius of the circle by typing the number in the Radius text box. Drag the circle around the Preview pane to place it properly.

The final option in the Action drop-down menu, Reset, is useful when you would like to clear the LCD screen of any items. The default NXT screen (which shows the name of the program currently running) will appear on the LCD screen.

Before closing out this chapter on the DISPLAY block, I want to cover one additional item briefly: data hubs (this topic will be covered in more detail in Chapter 7).

Data Hubs

Most programming blocks come with what's called a "data hub." Take a look at Figure 3-10.

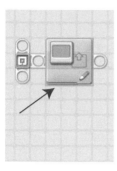

Figure 3-10. *Click on the DISPLAY block here, and the data hub will drop down.*

If you click the bottom-left edge of a block, this section will drop down and reveal the data hub (see Figure 3-11). Click the section again, and the data hub will close. It might take some practice to find the correct place to click, so try it a few times until you get used to opening and closing the data hub.

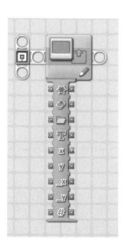

Figure 3-11. *The DISPLAY block's data hub can be used for more advanced programming.*

What is this data hub? The data hub allows you to draw *data wires* from one block to another using *data plugs*. Data wires and plugs will be covered in much more detail in Chapter 7, but for now, all you really need to know is that wires can connect blocks to share data. Data plugs are places on the block where you will connect wires. So there will be a data plug on one block with a wire going out and another data plug on a different block with a wire coming in. Data wires can carry information such as text, numbers, and other values. Remember all those items you could configure in the DISPLAY block? Well, items such as the text displayed or the radius of a circle can all be configured without using the configuration panel. Instead, you can draw data wires from one block's plugs into plugs on another block. I'll cover this topic in more detail later in the book (in Chapter 7), but right now, I just want you to take a look at Figure 3-12, so I can give you a preview of what's to come.

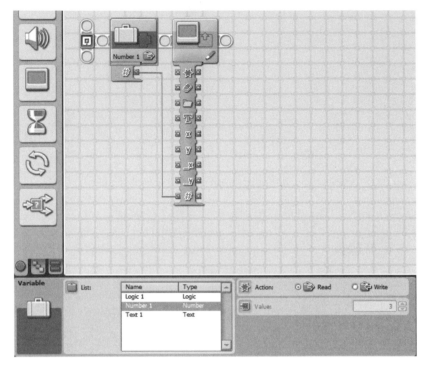

Figure 3-12. *An example of one DISPLAY block plug providing data to another block.*

In Figure 3-12, I've placed a VARIABLE block in front of the DISPLAY block. I cover the VARIABLE block in Chapter 18, but for now, all you really need to know is that this type of block can hold text, a number, or what's called a logic value (either True or False). In this example, I've configured the VARIABLE block to hold a number: 3.

Now, here's where it gets fun. Remember that when you draw a circle you can specify the radius of the circle in the configuration panel? Well, this VARIABLE block has only one plug in its data hub. For this block, it's holding the value of 3. I click that plug and draw a line into the last plug of the DISPLAY block's data hub. That last plug corresponds to the radius of a drawn circle (hover your mouse pointer over a plug, and it will tell you what it is). When I drag the wire *out* of the VARIABLE block plug and *into* the DISPLAY block plug, the line becomes solid yellow, and I know I've correctly configured the DISPLAY block.

■Note Plugs on the left side of a block's data hub are known as *input plugs*. Plugs on the right side of the block's data hub are called *output plugs*.

If the line is dotted, it tells me I've incorrectly connected two plugs. This can happen for many reasons. For example, if I had put text into the VARIABLE block and dragged the wire into the DISPLAY block's Radius plug, I would get a dotted line. This happens because the Radius plug expects a number value to be coming out of the VARIABLE block, not text.

As I mentioned earlier, I'll cover data plugs in more detail in Chapter 7. Before you begin using these data wires for more advanced programming, however, you need to understand the basics of the programming blocks.

Let's continue learning about blocks in Chapter 4 with the MOVE block.

CHAPTER 4

■ ■ ■

Get Movin'

I would say that the MOVE block is probably one of the most important blocks when it comes to programming a robot. Without the MOVE block, you can still build bots, but they won't be able to do much. They can sit on a desk or table (just like SPOT), but they're not going to be very exciting to watch. Any robot that you design that uses one or more motors will use the MOVE block.

So, let's go over this very important block and see what it can do.

The MOVE block

Open your Mindstorms NXT software, and drag and drop a MOVE block from the Common Palette onto the beam. The configuration panel will appear in the lower-left corner of the screen (see Figure 4-1).

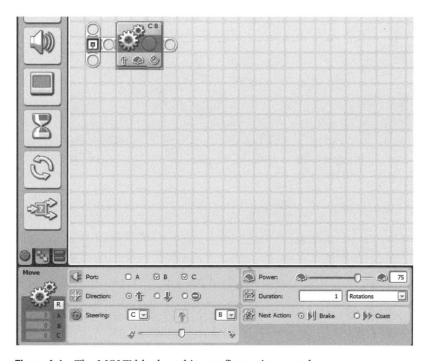

Figure 4-1. *The MOVE block and its configuration panel*

Your Brick has three ports for motors: Port A, Port B, and Port C. You must plug motors into these ports in order for them to work properly. Motors have numerous options including how fast they spin (Power) and how long or far they spin (Duration). By default, a MOVE block is configured to control Port B and Port C on the Brick. The other defaults include a Power setting of 75 and a Duration of 1 rotation, and the Next Action is set to Brake.

Moving Forward and Backward

Before I move on, I want to bring to your attention the subject of motor spin direction. Take a look at Figure 4-2. It shows a motor in two different orientations.

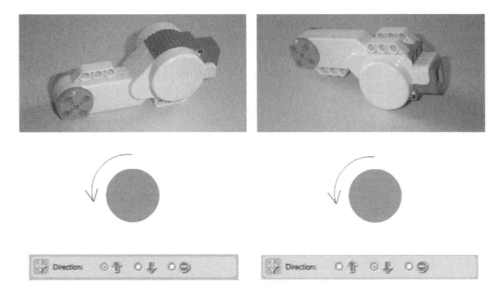

Figure 4-2. *A MOVE block can configure a motor to spin in two different directions (note the direction settings for each).*

All motors can spin forward and backward. But you need to be careful when describing a motor as "spinning forward" or "spinning backward," because the orientation of the motor also needs to be described. When we program, we have to take into consideration the orientation of the motor.

In Figure 4-2, the motor on the left has the up arrow selected in the Direction section on the MOVE block configuration panel. This up arrow corresponds to FORWARD, and this motor spins in the direction shown, counterclockwise. Now, if I flip this motor over (like the motor on the right side of Figure 4-2) but don't change the Direction arrow selection, the motor will spin in the opposite direction (clockwise). I have to change the Direction arrow to down (or REVERSE) to make the motor spin counterclockwise when it's position like the motor on the right.

Be sure to keep this in mind when building and programming your bots. Depending on whether you want your bot to move forward or backward, you'll have to select the proper Direction arrow (up or down) based on how the motors are attached to the bot.

Okay, now let's go over the rest of the MOVE block configuration panel.

First, we'll cover the ports. The MOVE block can control Ports A, B, and C and any motors attached to those ports. There is no rule for the way in which you connect motors to ports, but I would recommend that you decide on a "standard" method for connecting motors and stick with it for all robots you build.

As an example, look at Figure 4-3. When I build a robot I always connect the motor on the left side of the Brick (with the Brick's sensor ports on the bottom and motor ports on top) to Port B and the motor on the right side of the Brick to Port C. I always use Port A for my third motor. If I build a bot that doesn't need a third motor, Port A is always left open.

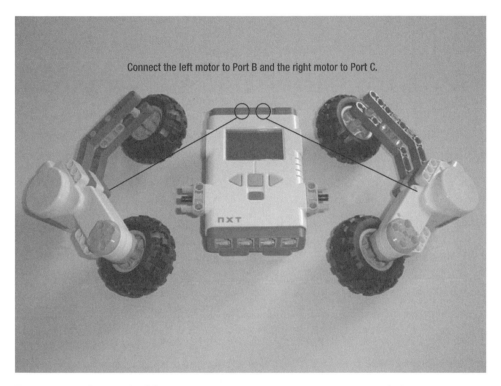

Figure 4-3. *Pick a method for connecting your motors to your ports, and always use it.*

When you connect a motor to a port, you must make certain to check the box for that Port in the MOVE block's configuration panel (see Figure 4-4). In Figure 4-4, you'll also notice that the motor ports you select (in this example, Ports A and B) are listed on the MOVE block in the upper right corner. This can be helpful for troubleshooting and to remind you which motors will be used.

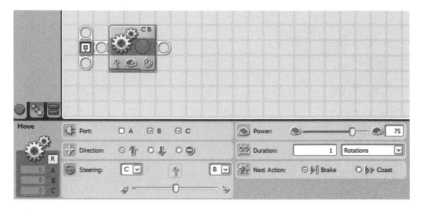

Figure 4-4. *Use the MOVE block's configuration panel to select motor ports.*

Stopping

I've already mentioned the Direction control using the up and down arrows (or FORWARD and REVERSE). The other option shown in Figure 4-5 is STOP. If you select the STOP option, check the Port boxes for the motor(s) you want to stop.

Figure 4-5. *Select the STOP option in the MOVE configuration panel to stop selected motors.*

Steering

The next item to discuss is steering. Figure 4-6 shows the Steering section that is available if you have selected either FORWARD or REVERSE for the Direction and have two motor ports checked.

Note If you select all three motor ports, the Steering control is turned off.

Figure 4-6. *The MOVE block's Steering control in the configuration panel*

The Steering control can be very useful if you know how to use it. Depending on its setting, you can configure a bot to move in a small or large circle or just spin in place.

If you have two motors configured for your bot's movement (Ports B and C, for example), you can make your bot spin in place by dragging the Steering control all the way to the left or right (the direction you drag the control will determine if the bot spins clockwise or counter-clockwise). Try it! Drag the slider all to the way to the left. Save your program, upload it to your bot, and run the program. Which direction did the bot spin? Now let's change it. Drag the slider all the way to the right. Save, upload, and run the program again. Did the bot spin in the opposite direction?

You can also program your bot to drive in a circle; the size of the circle depends on how far you drag the Steering control left or right: dragging it closer to either the far right or far left will make the circle smaller. You'll have to play around with the Steering control to get the size of the circle just the way you want it. Go ahead and try this, too. Drag the Steering slider to the left but not all the way. Upload the program, and run it. Did the bot move in a small or large circle? Try it again, but this time, move the Steering slider to a different location before you upload and run the program. Did the bot move in a smaller or larger circle?

Power Settings

Next on the configuration panel is the Power section (see Figure 4-7). The Power setting range is 0 to100. You can type a value into the Power text box or drag the sliding bar to the right (to decrease power) or to the left (to increase power).

Figure 4-7. *The MOVE block's Power setting has a range of 0 to 100.*

Most uses of the Power setting will involve increasing or decreasing the spin speed of a motor. But there is one additional consideration, that is, lifting or pushing strength. If your robot is lifting a heavy object, for example, you might need to set the Power setting to a higher value. The motor will not spin as fast as it would if there were no resistance, but you may find that you need that extra power for the motor to successfully lift the object. The same goes for pushing. To push an object, your bot might need a higher Power setting than it will if it's not pushing anything. Surface conditions also affect power; climbing a hill will take more power and possibly slow the robot. Likewise, going down a hill won't take as much power. Also, whether a surface is smooth or rough can affect power; for example, you need more power to move over carpet than wood flooring. This is one of those settings where you'll just have to experiment. Change the Power setting, and play around with the Steering slider. See how fast or slow you can program your bot to make a circle. This will give you a better understanding of how the Power setting will affect your future bots.

Duration Settings

The Duration section of the configuration panel offers the most control of the MOVE block. There are four options in the Duration drop-down menu: Unlimited, Degrees, Rotations, and Seconds (see Figure 4-8).

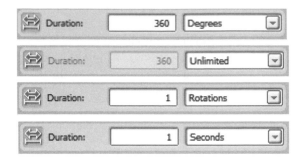

Figure 4-8. *There are four options for the Duration section of a MOVE block.*

From the Duration section, you can choose to have your motors spin forever by clicking the drop-down menu and choosing Unlimited. When the Duration is set to Unlimited, a single MOVE block will continue to spin its motors until the program ends or until you stop it. (There are other ways to stop a MOVE block such as using a LOOP block; I'll cover the LOOP block in Chapter 11.)

If you set the MOVE block Duration to Degrees, you must enter a value in the text box for the number of degrees for the motor(s) to spin. The value must be 0 or greater; it cannot be negative, but this limitation is simple to fix. If you wish for your motor to spin –90 degrees, for example, you simply type **90** in the text box and change the MOVE block Direction to its opposite setting (if it's set to spin FORWARD, just change it to REVERSE). If you've experimented with other programming environments, this may be unusual; it's possible you may have learned to use negative numbers to represent counterclockwise spinning of motors. Don't worry; you'll get used to the NXT-G method of simply changing the motor spin direction in the configuration panel. Just experiment with this concept, and it will start to make sense. Remember that your bot can spin a positive number of degrees, but you have to tell it whether to spin clockwise or counterclockwise by using the FORWARD or REVERSE directional controls.

If the Duration is set to Rotations, the same rules apply. You cannot enter a negative value for rotations, but any value of 0 and higher is acceptable. In order to spin the motor(s), a negative number of rotations, just change the Direction to its opposite setting (FORWARD or REVERSE). One thing you *can* do with Rotations is use fractional or decimal values. For example, you could configure a motor to spin 2.3 rotations or 50.9 rotations.

You may be wondering why you would ever want to configure a motor to spin 2.3 rotations. Well, I'll be covering that in this book's appendix when I show you how to program MOVE blocks for specific distances. For now, just keep in mind that your bots have the ability to move very small distances or very large distances with good accuracy, and it all depends on your ability to figure out exactly how many degrees or rotations to spin the motors (feel free to skip ahead to the appendix if you just can't wait).

The last option in the Duration section is Seconds. When you choose this option, you must specify the number of seconds for the MOVE block to spin a motor (or motors). For obvious reasons, you can't configure it for a negative value (say, –5 seconds). Just type in the number of seconds you want the motor(s) to spin, and you're finished.

Braking and Coasting

Now, take a look at Figure 4-9, which shows the last option you can configure for the MOVE block—the Next Action section. There are two options: Brake and Coast. If you select the Brake option, any motors connected to the ports you've configured will be stopped *fast* when the Duration you set expires (for example, after 10 seconds). Braking is useful if you need your bot to stop quickly and accurately at a specific point. However, keep in mind that this takes battery power.

Figure 4-9. *You can configure motors to brake or coast.*

But what if you're not concerned about your bot stopping accurately? Then choose the Coast option. When you choose this option, any motors connected to the ports you've configured will stop receiving power, but the bot's momentum may carry it a little further; that's why it's labeled Coast—your bot will be coasting for a little while. You definitely want to try this out! So let's do that with some pseudo-code: SPOT, move forward 10 rotations at a Power of 75 and then Brake.

The MOVE block I've configured for SPOT is shown in Figure 4-10. Notice that I've configured Duration for 10 Rotations and Power at 75, and I've selected the Brake option. SPOT is also using Ports B and C for its motors, and I want it to travel in a straight line, so I've left the Steering control alone.

Figure 4-10. *The braking pseudo-code has been converted to a NXT-G program for SPOT.*

Now, when I upload and run this program, SPOT rapidly moves forward 10 rotations (about 6 feet) and comes to a quick stop.

Let's try a different test: SPOT, move backward 720 degrees at a Power of 100, and then Coast.

This time, I want SPOT to move in reverse, and I want the motors in Ports B and C to spin for 720 degrees. I want him to move *very fast*, so I've set the Power setting to 100. I don't need him to stop at a specific point, so I'll let him coast to a stop. See Figure 4-11 for the block programming of the pseudo-code.

Figure 4-11. *A new coasting program for SPOT*

After I uploaded and ran this program, I watched as SPOT moved even faster in reverse for 720 degrees (about 15 inches). But this time, he didn't stop right away; he continued to roll for a few more inches, because I programmed him to coast to a stop.

Now, it's your turn. Using what you've learned in this chapter, create some different programs for your bot.

When you're finished, I have a final test for you to run before continuing on to Chapter 5: Program your bot to move forward for 10 rotations at a Power setting of 50, and set it to Brake. Place a piece of tape on the floor, and make this your bot's starting position. Now, run the program, and mark its stopping position with tape as well.

Next, run the same program, but change the Brake option to Coast. How far did it go beyond the previous stopping position?

Finally, reduce the Power setting a little bit, and run the program again (with the Coast option). How far did it go beyond the stopping position this time?

Keep reducing the Power setting and running the program until the bot stops at the original stopping position.

Why am I asking you to do this? Recall that I told you that the Brake option uses up battery power. This test shows you that you can save battery power by reducing the Power setting and keeping the Coast option. Running tests like this will help you to figure out how best to program your bot to save battery power and to correctly perform its programmed actions!

Okay, that's it for the MOVE block. Feel free to play around with the MOVE block until you're comfortable with it. Then, continue on to Chapter 5, where I cover the RECORD/PLAY block.

CHAPTER 5

■■■

Record and Play Back

One nice feature of the NXT-G programming language is the RECORD/PLAY block. With this block, you can record the movements of your bot's motors to a file that is stored on the Brick. This file can be used to later play back the bot's movement.

For this chapter, we'll use SPOT again. But this time, I'm going to add one additional motor (motor A) to make SPOT do something silly like spin an arm or a sensor around. Feel free to do what you like. My SPOT has motor B (in Port B) spinning the left wheel of my bot and motor C (in Port C) spinning the right wheel. I have motor A (in Port A) spinning a small propeller (like an airplane) on the front of the robot (see Figure 5-1).

Figure 5-1. *SPOT with his new propeller*

I'm ready to record some basic movement. If you've built your own version of SPOT, follow along. Here's how we will do it.

The RECORD/PLAY block is located on the Common Palette directly below the MOVE block. Drag and drop a RECORD/PLAY block on the beam (see Figure 5-2).

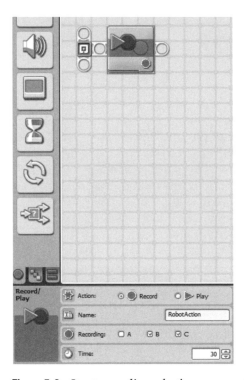

Figure 5-2. *Start recording a bot's movements with the RECORD/PLAY block.*

I know it seems like common sense, but I still need to say it: we cannot play back SPOT's recorded movements until we've actually recorded some. So the first thing we're going to need to do is configure the RECORD/PLAY block to record SPOT's movements. To do this, in the block's Action section, select the Record option as shown in Figure 5-3. This is the default setting when you drop a RECORD/PLAY block onto the workspace.

Figure 5-3. *First, choose the Record option in the Action section.*

Next, we need to specify a name for the recorded movement. As an example, I want SPOT to move forward 2 feet (motors B and C will be spinning forward) and turn left. I then want motor A to spin the propeller a few times. I'm going to type the words **Takeoff** in the Name text box shown in Figure 5-4, but you can type whatever description you like that will help you remember the purpose of the recorded movement.

Figure 5-4. *Give your recorded movement a unique name.*

The name you type in the Name text box is the name of a file that will be stored on the Brick. This file must be stored on the Brick in order for you to later play back the movement, so try to make the name memorable and easy to understand.

Now, look at Figure 5-5. The Recording section of the configuration panel is where you will specify which ports should be monitored. In my example, motors B and C will move my bot around, and motor A will spin the propeller. So I want to select all the ports. If you are not using one of the motor Ports, you don't need to select it. You won't get an error if you select a motor port and don't use it, however.

Figure 5-5. *Configure the motor ports to monitor and record.*

The last item you will need to configure is the amount of time (in seconds) you wish to record your bot's movements (see Figure 5-6). You can type in the number of seconds you want to record or click the up and down arrows with your mouse to select the number in the Time section.

Figure 5-6. *Enter the number of seconds to record in the Time section.*

You can record anywhere from 1 second up into the hundreds of hours. Is this realistic? Not really. Your NXT Brick has a limited amount of memory, and you'll find that you are limited to a few minutes at most. And even recording a few minutes of movement will probably not leave much memory for your actual program. You'll have to play around with the Time section to test its limits.

Once you've got your RECORD/PLAY block configured, save the program, and upload it to your NXT bot. Place the bot at its starting position, and press the Run button for your new program. Using your hands, guide the bot through the movements you wish your bot to perform.

For my example, I simply push the bot forward 2 feet and stop. I then turn the bot to the left and stop. Next, I spin the little propeller on the front of the bot 5 or 6 times, and I'm finished.

I suggest that you time your movements as you're doing them. If you come close to the number of seconds you configured, you can simply leave the recording time alone. If you didn't have enough time, go back and add the right number of seconds to your program, save it, and run it again to record the complete movements. Most importantly, if you originally configured *too much time*, reduce the number of seconds you entered in the Time section; because the recording process will continue to run until the time is over, the file stored on the Brick will be larger than it needs to be.

Okay, so you've successfully recorded your bot's movements, and there is a file stored on the Brick with the name you gave it in the Name section (you can verify this by connecting your Brick to your computer and checking its memory contents). Now, let me show you how to play back the file.

It's so easy, you're going to laugh. Create a new program, and drop in a RECORD/PLAY block. This time, however, select the Play option in the Action section (see Figure 5-7).

Figure 5-7. *Configure your bot to play back the recorded movement.*

The only other section that can be configured now is the Name section. Type the name of the file that contains the recorded movements in the Name section (see Figure 5-8). For my example, I've typed **Takeoff**, the name I gave the file that moves the bot forward 2 feet, turns it left, and then spins the propeller a few times.

Figure 5-8. *Enter the name of the file you created during the Record process.*

Next, you need to save the new program and upload it to your Brick. Before you run the program, place your bot in the original starting position (or wherever you like), and press the Run button to run the program. The bot will begin to move and will match the movements you recorded earlier. That's it for the RECORD/PLAY block.

Here are some ideas for using the RECORD/PLAY block:

- A fun use for it is to record your bot doing some sort of dance (for 10 to 20 seconds) and save it to a file called Dance. If you keep the Dance file on your brick, you can drop in a RECORD/PLAY block anywhere in your program and have your bot do the little dance (you can drop it in multiple times, too).

- Teams could use this block when giving a presentation. The bot might have interesting parts and mechanisms that you wish to focus attention on, and the RECORD/PLAY block could be used to let the audience view these more easily. Configure the times properly, and you can synchronize it to a speech given on the robot and its different components.

Chapter 6 will show you how to give your robot the ability to talk and make some noise!

CHAPTER 6

■ ■ ■

Make Some Noise!

Sound can be used to give a bot more personality. Think about how boring R2-D2 would be without all the chirps and whistles. Well, you can give your bot plenty to say by using the SOUND block. Sound isn't limited to just giving your bots character, though. Sounds can be useful as a way to judge your bot's progress through a maze, for example, with the bot programmed to issue specific sounds when it makes a left or encounters a dead end. Read on for all the details on the SOUND block.

The SOUND Block

When you drop in the SOUND block on the beam, you are given access to the configuration panel shown in Figure 6-1.

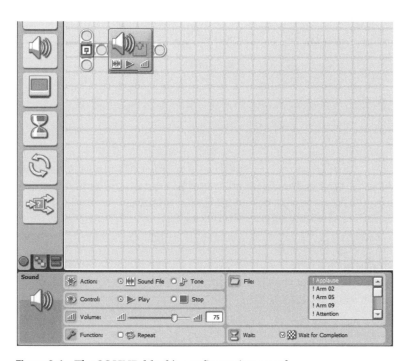

Figure 6-1. *The SOUND block's configuration panel*

Action Settings

The first section I want to cover is the Action section. You have two options: Sound File or Tone.

Sound File

Select the Sound File option, and take a look at Figure 6-2. See the section called File? Clicking the Sound File option opens the File section; the File section contains a large collection of prerecorded sounds that your bot can play through the Brick's speaker. Click one of the sound files, and if your computer has speakers, you will hear the sound file play.

Figure 6-2. *The Sound File option allows you to select a sound from the File section.*

Tone

Now, select the other option, Tone. Notice that the File section changes to a section called Note (see Figure 6-3).

Figure 6-3. *The Tone option allows you to specify tones from the Note section.*

Note Settings

The Note section provides you with a few options. The easiest option is to simply click one of the piano keys. You will hear the tone played if your computer has speakers attached. Notice that when you click on a key, the note you click is displayed in the text box above the keys in the form of a letter: A, B, C, D, E, F, or G (with sharps for the black keys).

The other option available in the Note section is the ability to specify how long the note will play. Type a number in the text box for the number of seconds to play the note.

That covers the Action section; the remaining sections for the SOUND block (Control, Volume, Function, and Wait) are the same whether you choose the Sound File or Tone option. Now, let me explain each of these remaining sections.

Control Settings

The second section on the SOUND block is Control. This section has two options: Play and Stop (see Figure 6-4).

Figure 6-4. *The Control section of the SOUND block*

The Play option is simple. Select it, and any sound file or tone you selected in the Action section will play. Not too difficult, right?

The Stop option requires a little more explanation. To do this, I need to jump ahead to the Function section (see Figure 6-5).

Figure 6-5. *The Function section of the SOUND block*

Function Settings

The Function section only has one option: Repeat. If the box is checked, the Sound File or Tone will continue to play until your program ends *or* until another SOUND block is reached with the Stop option selected in the Control section. If the box is unchecked, the sound file or tone will only play *one* time.

So, you can see that the Stop option is useful *only* when you have another SOUND block that is continually playing.

Volume Settings

OK, now for the Volume section. You can see in Figure 6-6 that the Volume control can be changed either by using the slider or by typing a value (0 to 100) in the text box. You will have to experiment with the Volume control to determine what works best for your robots, but keep in mind that loud sounds will use up more battery power than sounds played at a lower volume.

Figure 6-6. *The Volume section of the SOUND block*

Wait Settings

The last section in the SOUND block is the Wait section (see Figure 6-7). When you have selected a sound file or tone to play and the Repeat box (in the Function section) is not checked, the Wait for Completion checkbox is available.

Figure 6-7. *The Wait section of the SOUND block*

If you place a check in the Wait for Completion box, the Sound File or Tone you choose will play completely before any further programming blocks are executed. Let me give you an example using pseudo-code: SPOT, play me a C note for 10 seconds and then move forward 5 rotations.

Now, here's how I will convert the pseudo-code into a NXT-G program. First, I drop in a SOUND block and configure it to play a C note for 10 seconds (see Figure 6-8). I'm going to leave the Wait for Completion box unchecked and set the Volume to 75.

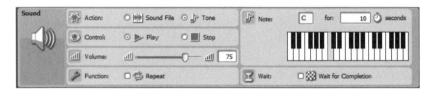

Figure 6-8. *SPOT will first play a C note for 10 seconds.*

Next, I'm going to drop in a MOVE block (see Figure 6-9). I'll configure this MOVE block to spin motor B and motor C FORWARD for 5 rotations and then Brake. I'm also going to set Power at 50.

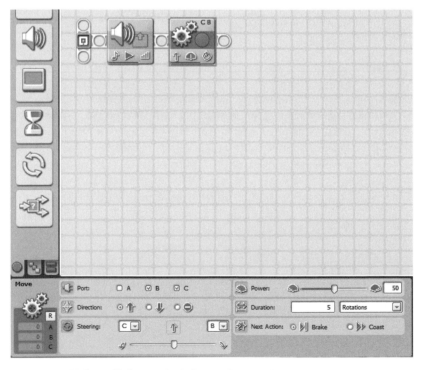

Figure 6-9. *SPOT will then MOVE forward 5 rotations.*

Next, I save the program, upload it to SPOT, and run it. Go ahead and create and run this same program on your bot. What happens?

Well, I pressed the Run button and the C note started to play. But before the C note stopped, motors B and C started spinning. What happened?

Go back to Figure 6-8, and notice that the Wait For Completion box is unchecked. This means that when the SOUND block starts playing, the program will continue to the MOVE block that spins the motors. But that's not what I wanted SPOT to do. Take a look again at the pseudo-code: SPOT, play a C note for 10 seconds and *then* move forward 5 rotations.

I wanted SPOT to play the C note for 10 seconds before moving forward. To do this, I simply need to go back to my SOUND block and check the Wait for Completion box. This will tell SPOT to wait until the SOUND block is finished (10 seconds) before continuing with the program. So, I make this change (see Figure 6-10) and run the program again.

Figure 6-10. *Making one change to the SOUND block will fix the problem.*

This time, SPOT does exactly what I wanted him to do. He plays the C note for 10 seconds, and when the SOUND block is finished, motors B and C spin, and SPOT moves forward 5 rotations. Perfect!

Now you can add sound files and tones to your robots to give them more personality. But before we finish this chapter, let me also tell you that sounds can be used when testing your robots. For example, in a complex program you can drop in a SOUND block to let you know when the robot has reached a certain portion of the program. Let's say you want to know when your robot has reached the part of a program where it has to decide between turning left and turning right. You could place a SOUND block directly in front of the MOVE blocks and program a sound to play when turning left and a different sound for turning right. After you've tested and verified the program is working properly, you can remove the SOUND blocks and run the program normally. In this example, SOUND blocks give you an idea of where a robot's program is currently executing by giving you an audible alert, which is very useful for troubleshooting and testing.

Now, before we investigate any new blocks, I want to go over the different ways your robots receive input—this includes motors, sensors, timers, and the buttons on the Brick. Chapter 7 covers all of this, so read on!

CHAPTER 7

■ ■ ■

Wired!

Some of the questions I hear the most are related to data hubs and wires—and for good reason! A block's data hub can be confusing, especially when a block has numerous options on the hub. And wires can be just as difficult to figure out.

In this chapter, I want to take a short break from learning about NXT-G programming blocks and give you some background and tips on how to use data hubs and wires. I hope that any confusion you have will be cleared up by the end of this chapter.

Passing Around Information

To help you understand hubs and wires, let me start with a fake programming block called the COLOR block. This block is shown in Figure 7-1.

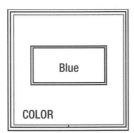

Figure 7-1. *The COLOR block*

This imaginary block is one of the simplest blocks you'll ever encounter. It can hold *one* color. This block holds Blue. It will always hold Blue and nothing else. There is no way to change the color. There's even worse news—the block has no way of sharing this color with a robot. It's a very boring and useless block.

What would make this block useful to us? Well, first, it would be nice to be able to change the color. My favorite color is green, so I'd at least like to change the block to a Green block. I might not be able to do anything else with the block at this point, but at least it will contain my favorite color!

One of the things the block lacks is a way to get inside the block and change Blue to Green. What's so great about creating the COLOR block is that I can change it whenever I like (because it's a fake block). The first thing I'm going to do is attach a very small color keyboard to the block so I can change the color. This color keyboard is a strange type of keyboard, though; it will only let me type colors. If I try to type in "Jim" or "five," the keyboard will buzz to let me know that it's not going to cooperate. Take a look at the updated COLOR block in Figure 7-2.

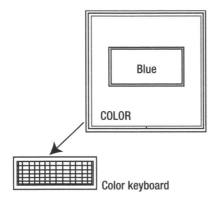

Figure 7-2. *I've added a fake color keyboard, so I can change the Blue block to a Green block.*

Perfect! Now I can type Green. Later, if I want to change to Yellow or Red, I can simply type the new color, and the block will change.

Now I've changed the color, and I have a Green block. Other than looking at it, there's really not much I can do with it. Just like I added a small keyboard to the block, I think I'll now connect a small, fake color screen to the block that will take whatever color is stored inside and display it. This screen is just like my weird keyboard; it will only display a color. (If I had a "direction screen" and I connected it to the block, it wouldn't know what to do with a color. But if I connected it to a DIRECTION block that holds North, East, West, or South, then it would definitely work!)

Figure 7-3 shows my new color screen connected to the Green block.

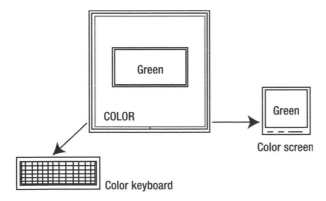

Figure 7-3. *The color screen lets me see what color is stored in the COLOR block.*

So, let's review how this works: the COLOR block can hold only *one* color, not a number or a day or a name.

Next, the COLOR block has a color keyboard attached. I can change the color the COLOR block holds but only by using this special keyboard, and this keyboard will let me type in *only* colors.

Finally, I've attached a color screen to the COLOR block. This special screen will only display colors and nothing else, not names or types of food.

If I detach the color keyboard, can I still display the color inside? Yes, but only if I keep the color screen attached.

If I detach the color screen, can I still change the color inside the block? Yes, again, but only if I keep the color keyboard attached.

Let me give you another way to describe this COLOR block:

- The COLOR block will accept a color as input from the keyboard.

- The COLOR block will also provide a color as output to the screen.

There are some programming words for you in that description: input and output. When thinking about blocks, always remember that any information that is provided to a block is *input*. Any information that the block can give out (share) can be considered *output*.

Now, let's look at a block with a few more options. Take a look at the fake CUP block in Figure 7-4.

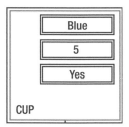

Figure 7-4. *The CUP block is a little more complex.*

The CUP block can hold three pieces of information: the cup's Color, its Height in inches, and a Yes answer if the cup is empty or a No answer if the cup is not empty. Now, here's where it gets fun.

Take a look at Figure 7-5. The COLOR block has an easier way for me to provide input to the block and to receive output from the block. It's called a *hub*.

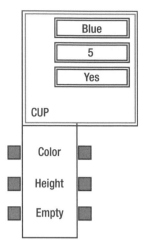

Figure 7-5. *The CUP block has a hub for connecting things.*

You can see in the figure that there are three input plugs on the left side of the hub and three output plugs on the right side. These are where I will plug in keyboards, screens, and other items.

Just like the COLOR block, though, the CUP block is very picky about what types of devices are connected to it. For the Color input plug, I can only connect something that supplies a color. We already know that a color keyboard will work. I could connect a color keyboard and change the color of the cup from Blue to Green. But there's a better way!

Remember that COLOR block we played around with earlier? Well, it has a data hub, too; it was just hidden inside the block. If I click on the lower left edge of the COLOR block, the COLOR block's hub will pop down; this is shown in Figure 7-6.

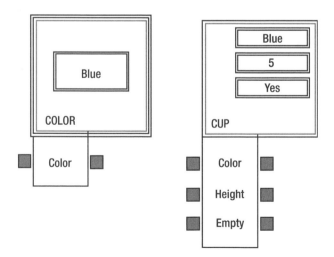

Figure 7-6. *The COLOR block also has a hub.*

The input plug on the left side of the COLOR block is where I can plug in a color keyboard to change the color inside the block. The output plug on the right can be connected to a color screen, but in truth, it can be connected to any *input* plug that can accept a color. Notice the CUP block has an input plug that will accept a color! So instead of connecting a color keyboard to the CUP block, I can use a simple wire to connect the output plug on the COLOR block to the input plug on the CUP block (see Figure 7-7).

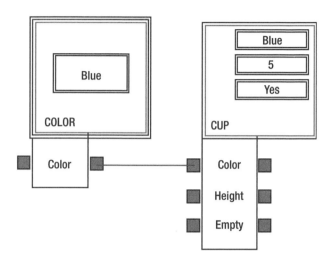

Figure 7-7. *I'll connect a wire from the COLOR block to the CUP block.*

I can also connect a height keyboard that can only be used to type in a cup's height in inches. If I try to type in anything besides a number, the keyboard won't work. I'll also connect a logic keyboard to the Empty input plug. A logic keyboard is a very special keyboard—it can only be used to provide Yes or No answers. Not Maybe or Sometimes; only Yes or No.

What I would like to do with the CUP block is to connect it to a screen that will display one of two things (but not both):

- Fill the [Color] cup with [Height] inches of water.

- The [Color] cup is not empty.

To do this, I can use a screen to print the color and height that are provided by the CUP block (Figure 7-8 shows my setup so far).

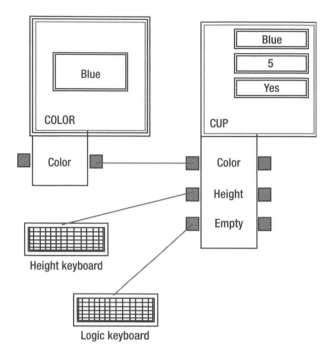

Figure 7-8. *Everything is hooked up and ready to use.*

But before I print the color and height, I need another special block that can examine the contents of the cup and determine if it is empty or not empty. Now, all I need to do is reveal my new EXAMINE block, shown in Figure 7-9.

The EXAMINE block can perform a nice trick. It takes a Yes or No answer (logic) and, depending on the answer, performs action 1 or action 2. Action 1 will occur if the answer is Yes; Action 2 will occur if the answer is No (for more information on logic and the LOGIC block, feel free to jump ahead to Chapter 8).

I can use this block to examine the contents of the CUP block. It will first look at the data plug labeled Empty. If the data the Empty data plug provides is Yes, the EXAMINE block will use the "EXAMINE = Yes" screen. If the data is No, the block will use the "EXAMINE = No" screen.

Figure 7-9 shows that when this program is run, the screen will display "Fill the Blue cup with 5 inches of water." It does this because the EXAMINE block receives the Yes data from the CUP block. It then performs the actions required for a Yes answer.

If I go back and change the Color to Yellow and the Height of the cup to 3 (using a color keyboard and height keyboard), this information will be passed from the CUP block to the EXAMINE block. If I change the logic answer from Yes to No using the logic keyboard, the EXAMINE block will receive the No data from the CUP block and perform the action required for a No answer: the screen displays "The Yellow cup is not empty."

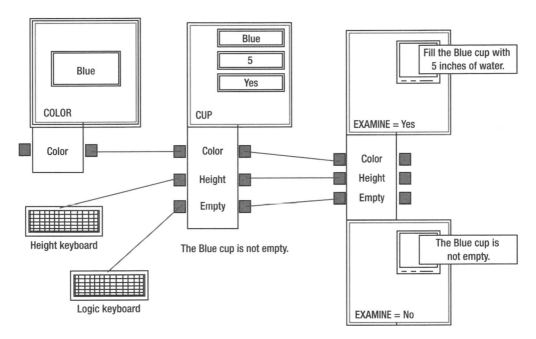

Figure 7-9. *The new EXAMINE block*

There are many more fake blocks that I could create, but I hope you're starting to understand how blocks can receive input data and provide output data. Both types of data (input and output) can be provided by you (by typing information in or selecting options in a configuration panel), or the data can be provided by other blocks using wires.

One thing you also need to know is that some blocks might not have any input plugs; some blocks might not have any output plugs, and a few, rare blocks have no data plugs at all.

You'll also be happy to hear this bit of information: I've created a bunch of fake blocks that can only accept color or height (and I could create a *bunch* of fake types of input), but you're fortunate, because when it comes to NXT-G, you only need to know about three types of data:

- *Text*: Letters, words, sentences, and even numbers can be considered text.

- *Number*: Numbers can be positive or negative, and sometimes they are limited to integers (only numbers like –3, 0, 4, 8, or 10 and no numbers with decimal points like 4.3 or 8.5).

- *Logic*: This can be Yes or No (another way to say it is True or False).

When you are programming, the only data that can be passed to and from a block are text, numbers, and logic types (Yes/No or True/False)—only these three! And just as your CUP block wouldn't let you use a logic keyboard to type in the color, a block's input and output data plugs will be very picky about the types of data they accept. You'll find an NXT-G block with plugs that accept Text and Logic, but no Number plug. Another NXT-G block will have no input plugs but maybe two output plugs that only provide Number data.

The good news is that if you ever drag a wire from one plug to an incompatible plug (if you try to drag a wire from a Text plug to a Logic plug, for example), the wire will be *broken*. By that,

I mean that the wire will become a dashed gray line indicating that you made a mistake. If you correctly connected a wire, the wire will have a color:

- The wire is yellow for the Number data type.

- The wire is orange for the Text data type.

- The wire is green for the Logic data type.

- If the wire is gray (and dashed), the wire is broken and will not work.

It takes practice to drag and connect wires from plug to plug. Sometimes, the wires will do strange things and go off in strange directions. You'll just have to play around with them until you figure out how to control them properly.

Well, now it's time to get back to real NXT-G blocks. You'll see in the figures I provide that many times I'll have a block's data hub opened. If you hover the mouse pointer over a data plug, it will show you the name of the data plug (something like Empty or Height in my examples).

For some of the plugs, it's fairly easy to figure out what type of data type they use (the Number plug requires the, duh, Number data type). Others aren't so easy to figure out. You can either check the help documentation, which provides a detailed description of a block's data hub plugs along with the types of data they accept *or* you can just experiment and drag some wires to it; the color of the wire will tell you if you're correct, or a gray wire will tell you to try again.

My last bit of good news is that you cannot ruin a program with incorrect wires! If you connect a wire that's incompatible, just click the input end of the wire (a wire always has an input end and an output end), and the wire will disappear. No worries!

This is a *lot* of information to absorb, and you've only scratched the surface of what wires can do for you. But there's *power* in wires! Wires can save you time by allowing you to use existing data over and over again; wires can be split, meaning you can split one wire and provide two different blocks with the same data! Wires can also go in the other direction, so you can send an output wire from the end of your program all the way back to an input plug at the start of your program! Keep your eyes open throughout this book to learn some new ways to use wires. Experiment on your own, and you'll discover even more uses for wires.

OK, up next in Chapter 8 is a short discussion on a method robots use for making decisions using Yes and No answers.

CHAPTER 8

■■■

True or False?

What is the difference between the following two questions:

- What color is the sky?

- Is the sky blue?

Well, there are a *lot* of differences: the first question has five words and the second one has four words, for example. My real point in asking these two questions is to point out that the first question is open-ended; the sky could be blue, or gray, or any number of answers. The second question, however, only has two possible answers: yes or no.

When it comes to programming your robots, you need to understand that many times your robots can only *provide* you with those two answers: yes or no. At other times, your robots can *understand* only a yes or no answer. Understanding how to take a yes/no answer and use it to properly program your bots is the focus of this short chapter.

One or the Other

Let's have a question/answer session with SPOT:

Me: SPOT, what color is the box in front of you?

[SPOT sits there and gives no response.]

Me: SPOT, what is the position of your Touch sensor button?

[SPOT still sits there and gives no response.]

Hmmm . . . SPOT doesn't seem to be to responsive today. I seem to remember, however, that SPOT prefers yes/no questions, so let me try this again:

Me: SPOT, is the color of the box in front of you blue?

SPOT: Yes *[appears on the LCD screen]*

Me: SPOT, is your Touch sensor button pressed?

SPOT: No *[appears on the LCD screen]*

OK, now we're getting somewhere. SPOT does prefer to communicate with me using yes or no answers. Another way of saying this is that SPOT prefers to communicate using *logical responses*; a logical response is simply Yes or No.

■**Note** Some computers and robots use True or False, but it's all the same: Yes = True and No = False. Some computers and robots even use 1 or 0 as a logical response, where 1= True and 0 = False. There's even another method: On or Off! In that case, On = True and Off = False. But for the purposes of this chapter and programming, let's stick with either Yes/No or True/False.

Let's have another conversation with SPOT:

Me: SPOT, is your Ultrasonic sensor detecting an object 6 inches in front of you?

SPOT: True.

Me: SPOT, is your Right button being pressed?

SPOT: False.

Apparently, SPOT's sensors have the ability to return a logical response to SPOT that he can pass along to me. SPOT listens to his sensors' conditions and responds with True or False.

What does all this have to do with programming, though? Here's your answer: your NXT robots can send and receive logical responses to and from the sensors, motors, buttons, and other items.

As an example, take a look at Figure 8-1.

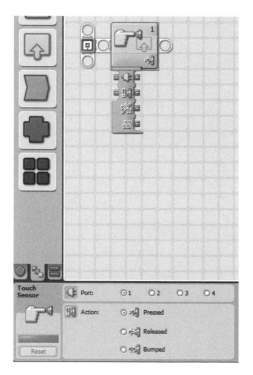

Figure 8-1. *The Touch sensor's configuration panel*

What you are looking at in Figure 8-1 is the TOUCH SENSOR block and its configuration panel. Notice also that the TOUCH SENSOR block has its data hub visible (see Chapter 7 for a discussion on data hubs and Chapter 9 for a more detailed discussion of the sensors). If you are only seeing one data output plug on the data hub, click the data hub again to expand it to its full size.

On the data hub, you'll see some small input and output data plugs. If you hover the mouse pointer over the third plug from the top, the words "Yes/No" will appear. What this tells you is that this data plug can provide output (using a data wire) in the form of a Logic data type.

But how do you know if the output will be Yes or No? Simple—the answer is based on what you are monitoring with the sensor.

In Figure 8-1, notice that the Touch sensor's Action section has the Pressed option selected. This means that if the Touch sensor's button is pressed down (and not released) the Yes/No Logic plug would provide a Yes answer. If the button is not pressed, the Yes/No Logic plug will provide a No answer.

Think back to Chapter 7; I told you that when you connect two blocks with a wire, the input and output data plugs *must* be carrying the same data type. In this case, if you wish to connect a wire from the Yes/No data plug, it must be going into a block that has a Logic data type input plug.

As an example, take a look at the new block in Figure 8-2.

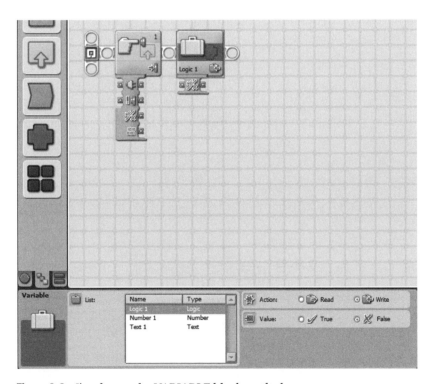

Figure 8-2. *I've dropped a VARIABLE block on the beam.*

This new block is a VARIABLE block. I cover this block in more detail in Chapter 18, but for now all you need to know about the VARIABLE block is that it can hold one of the three data types: Logic, Number, or Text. In Figure 8-2, I've configured the VARIABLE block to hold a Logic value. I've also opened the data hub, so you can see that it has a Yes/No input data plug. All that I need to do is connect it to the TOUCH SENSOR block with a wire (see Figure 8-3).

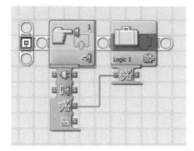

Figure 8-3. *Connecting two blocks with a wire*

When connecting blocks in a program using data wires, always keep in mind that a data wire will *only* work if it is connected to an input and output plug that expect the same data type (Logic, Number, or Text). I also need to point out that many blocks hold either a True or False value as a default setting. For example, the VARIABLE block in Figure 8-2 is configured to hold a default value of False. But you could easily change this to True (I've got more examples later in this book where you'll configure True/False values).

The Logic data type can be found in many blocks, especially the sensor blocks (see Figure 8-4). The sensor blocks all have a data plug that provides a Yes/No response. These plugs are designated by a check mark and an "X" that symbolize the Yes/No response.

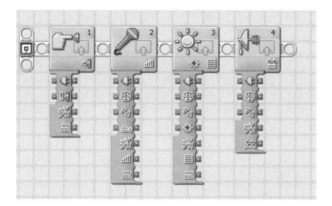

Figure 8-4. *The four sensors (Touch, Sound, Light, and Ultrasonic) all have Logic data plugs.*

Where the Logic data type really comes in handy, however, is with the LOOP and SWITCH blocks (these are covered in Chapters 11 and 12, respectively). Logic data types are very useful when programming a bot to make decisions on its own, and the LOOP and SWITCH blocks can both use a Yes/No response (as input) to give your robots more complex behaviors and control of itself. The bot can examine a sensor or motor or other type of input and, based on the Yes/No response, make further decisions about what it does next.

And that's it for this short chapter on logic. As I said, you'll get a more detailed description of how to use the Logic data type with the LOOP and SWITCH blocks in Chapters 11 and 12. Now let's change direction in Chapter 9 and take a look at some more items that can be used to communicate with the NXT Brick: sensors, buttons, and timers.

■■■

Feedback

Your LEGO Mindstorms NXT kit comes with a collection of motors and sensors. And the NXT Brick has three built-in timers plus the buttons on the Brick. Would it surprise you to learn that all of these items are able to provide some sort of feedback to the NXT Brick? The sensors are a little obvious; a sensor is designed to respond to external conditions such as light, touch, or sound and report this information to the Brick. But what about motors? And how can a timer be used as input or feedback to the Brick? All these questions have answers, and this chapter provides them.

What's Your Condition?

Let's start with the word *condition*. A traffic light has three conditions: red, yellow, and green. A light switch has two conditions: on and off. Just using these two simple examples, I can give you some pseudo-code for SPOT:

Me: SPOT, move forward until the traffic light turns red.

Me: SPOT, display the words "Light On" on your LCD screen until the light switch is off.

In both these examples, I'm assuming that SPOT has eyes and can see the traffic light or light switch. If SPOT doesn't have eyes, then I would need a way for the traffic light or light switch to provide their conditions to SPOT. The traffic light and light switch could then provide feedback, or input, to SPOT.

Asking a traffic light to provide input isn't realistic, but your NXT robots do have the ability to receive feedback from items such as the sensors. So I can change the pseudo-code for SPOT:

Me: SPOT, move forward until the Light sensor reports a value of 20.

Me: SPOT, display the word "Hello" until the Touch sensor reports that it has been pressed and released.

Me: SPOT, play a C note when the Ultrasonic sensor detects an object 6 inches in front of you.

The motors, too, can provide feedback:

Me: SPOT, spin motor A until motor B reports that it has spun 10 degrees.

Me: SPOT, display "5 rotations" when motor C has rotated five times.

I mentioned that the Brick has three built-in timers plus three buttons that can be used, so I could also write the following pseudo-code:

Me: SPOT, when 20 seconds have elapsed, turn 90 degrees.

Me: SPOT, play a B note if I press the left button and a C note if I press the right button.

Okay, so you can see that the sensors, motors, buttons, and timers can provide input to the Brick to control other actions (MOVE, SOUND, and other blocks). You program your robot to perform specific actions based on the conditions of these items. Just like you know a light switch has two conditions, on and off, you need to know the various conditions that the sensors, buttons, timers, and motors possess and can report to the Brick.

So, for the rest of this chapter, I'm going to explain the settings for these items, so you'll know how to configure them properly. Future blocks that we'll cover, including the WAIT, LOOP, and SWITCH blocks, will depend on your understanding of how to properly configure the conditions.

The method I'm going to use to do this is fairly simple: I'll describe each item (sensor, motor, button, and so on) and provide a description of the settings that can be modified within the item's configuration panel. Please note that I am also providing information on the so-called *legacy* items: the previous version of Mindstorms (Robotics Invention System, or RIS) included motors, sensors, and a lamp. These RIS items can be used with NXT robots but require special converter cables to connect to the NXT Brick. I call them "legacy" because they come from the older Mindstorms system, but they are still very useful and fully compatible with the NXT system.

■Note Right now, *only* the Education version of the NXT kit comes with software support for the legacy/RCX items. If you are running the Retail version, you may download NXT programming blocks for the RCX motors and sensors by visiting http://mindstorms.lego.com/Support/Updates/ and downloading the files from the Legacy Block Library section.

Configuring the Sensors

Let's start with the sensors—NXT Touch, RIS Touch, NXT Sound, NXT Light, RIS Light, NXT Ultrasonic, NXT Rotation, RIS Rotation, and RIS Temperature—which have some interesting rules to abide by.

First, sensors detect a change in a condition. The condition could be a change in light level, a change in volume (sound), or maybe a change in position (movement). The sensor is simply "watching" the changes in its condition. The Light sensor, for example, can detect changes in the level of lighting in the room.

Second, sensor programming blocks can *only* respond to one condition at a time. When you drop a sensor block into an NXT-G program, it has to be configured to test one condition. A single Light sensor, for example, cannot be configured to respond to whether the light in a room is below 80 *and* greater than 50. In order to test both conditions, you would need to use two Light sensor blocks in your program.

Finally, sensors can provide only a Logic type response: True or False. Think of our traffic light for a moment. Let's assume that every car has special traffic light sensors mounted on top. These light sensors are programmed to examine the conditions of the traffic light. Cars will move while the light is green and stop when the light is red. If the light is yellow, the car will slow down.

These traffic light sensors, then, can detect one of three possible conditions: green, yellow, or red. An NXT sensor can only check *one* condition, so if this were an NXT traffic light sensor, each car would require three traffic light sensors:

- If the first traffic light sensor detects green, the car should keep moving.

- If the second traffic light sensor detects yellow, the car should start slowing down.

- If the third traffic light sensor detects red, the car should stop.

Notice that *only* one condition can be true at any given time; the light cannot be green and red at the same time. So when the sensor detecting green is triggered, yellow and red cannot be triggered. Therefore, we can examine a sensor's Logic data type for a True/False response to the condition the sensor is configured to monitor.

Let's take a look now at the sensors.

NXT Touch Sensor

The NXT Touch sensor's configuration panel is shown in Figure 9-1.

Figure 9-1. *The NXT Touch sensor's configuration panel*

In the Port section, select the port where the NXT Touch sensor has been connected. The default port for the Touch sensor is Port 1.

In the Action section, you can select Pressed, Released, or Bumped. Remember that Bumped means quickly pressing and releasing the button—less than .5 seconds for the entire press-and-release action.

The NXT Touch sensor's data hub is shown in Figure 9-2. Remember that you can hover your mouse pointer over a data plug to obtain the plug's name.

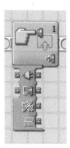

Figure 9-2. *The NXT Touch sensor's data hub*

The port number can be configured using the Port data plug and a Number data type wire with an input value of 1, 2, 3, or 4. This value can also be used as output by dragging a data wire out of the output Port data plug.

The Action data plug can use a Number data type with an input value of 0 for Pressed, 1 for Released, or 2 for Bumped.

The Yes/No data plug can provide an output value of True or False.

The Raw Value data plug can provide an output Number value with a range of 0–1024.

For the remaining blocks in this chapter, I will not be describing the blocks' data hubs—only the blocks' configuration panels (I simply wanted to show you that the sensor blocks can use their data hubs for even more options).

Click the Help menu, and select the "Contents and Index" option to view the Help files. Select a programming block from the left side of the screen (see Figure 9-3). Details for the block's data hub can be found at the bottom of that block's Help documentation (also shown in Figure 9-3). You can always consult this Help documentation to determine the data types for the various data plugs (Number, Logic, or Text).

Sound Sensor Block
Temperature* Sensor Block
Timer Block
Touch Sensor Block
Touch* Sensor Block
Ultrasonic Sensor Block
– Flow Blocks
Loop Block
Stop Block
Switch Block

This chart shows the different characteristics of the plugs on the Touch Sensor block's data hub:

	Plug	Data Type	Possible Range	What the Values Mean	This Plug is Ignored When...
	Port	Number	1 - 4	1 = Port 1, 2 = Port 2, 3 = Port 3, 4 = Port 4	
	Action	Number	0 - 2	0 = Pressed 1 = Released 2 = Bumped	
	Yes / No	Logic	True/False	Result of comparison	
	Raw Value	Number	0 - 1024	Raw (unscaled) value read from sensor	

Figure 9-3. *Touch Sensor Block is selected on the left and the Data Hub details are shown on the right.*

RIS Touch Sensor

The legacy RIS Touch sensor's configuration panel is shown in Figure 9-4.

Figure 9-4. *The RIS Touch sensor's configuration panel*

In the Port section, select the port where the RIS Touch sensor has been connected. The default port for the Touch sensor is Port 1.

In the Action section, you can select Pressed, Released, or Bumped.

NXT Sound Sensor

The NXT Sound sensor's configuration panel is shown in Figure 9-5.

Figure 9-5. *The NXT Sound sensor's configuration panel*

In the Port section, select the port where the NXT Sound sensor has been connected. The default port for the Sound sensor is Port 2.

In the Compare section, you must configure the sound value (0–100) as well as whether the sensor will monitor for sounds less than or greater than the configured value. You can use the drag bar to select the value or enter a numeric value in the range of 0–100 in the text box. Select the less than option (<) or the greater than option (>) from the drop-down menu *or* click the left or right radio button to configure this option.

NXT Light Sensor

The NXT Light sensor's configuration panel is shown in Figure 9-6.

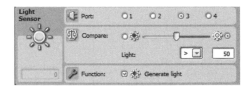

Figure 9-6. *The NXT Light sensor's configuration panel*

In the Port section, select the port where the NXT Light sensor has been connected. The default port for the Light sensor is Port 3.

In the Compare section, you must configure the light value (0–100) as well as whether the sensor will monitor for a light value less than or greater than the configured value. You can use the drag bar to select the value or enter a numeric value in the range of 0–100 in the text box. Select the less than option (<) or the greater than option (>) from the drop-down menu, or click on the left or right radio button to configure this option.

If you leave the "Generate light" box checked, the Light sensor will turn on its built-in LED to provide an artificial light source for assisting with determining light levels. If you uncheck the box, the Light sensor will only detect *ambient light levels*—that is, normal light conditions.

RIS Light Sensor

The RIS Light sensor's configuration panel is shown in Figure 9-7.

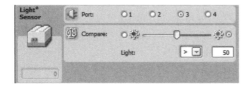

Figure 9-7. *The RIS Light sensor's configuration panel*

In the Port section, select the port where the RIS Light sensor has been connected. The default port for the Light sensor is Port 3.

In the Compare section, you must configure the light value (0–100) as well as whether the sensor will monitor for a light value less than or greater than the configured value. You can use the drag bar to select the value or enter a numeric value in the range of 0–100 in the text box. Select the less than option (<) or the greater than option (>) from the drop-down menu, or click the left or right radio button to configure this option.

NXT Ultrasonic Sensor

The NXT Ultrasonic sensor's configuration panel is shown in Figure 9-8.

Figure 9-8. *The Ultrasonic sensor's configuration panel*

In the Port section, select the port where the NXT Ultrasonic sensor has been connected. The default port for the Ultrasonic sensor is Port 4.

In the Compare section, you must configure the Distance value as well as whether the sensor will monitor for a distance value less than or greater than the configured value. You can use the drag bar to select the value in the range of 0–100, or you may type a value in the text box with a lower limit of 0 but an upper value greater than 100. Using the drag bar limits you to a range of 0-100, but you are able to type in a value greater than 100. Select the less than option (<) or the greater than option (>) from the drop-down menu, *or* click on the left or right radio button to configure this option.

In the Show section, select either Centimeters or Inches from the drop-down menu.

NXT Rotation Sensor

The NXT Rotation sensor's configuration panel is shown in Figure 9-9. Remember that the Rotation sensor is built into the NXT motors, so don't go looking for an actual NXT Rotation sensor by itself.

Figure 9-9. *The NXT Rotation sensor's configuration panel*

In the Port section, select the motor port where the NXT motor (Rotation sensor) has been connected. The default port for the Rotation sensor is Port A.

In the Action section, you should select the Read option if you want the built-in rotation sensor to monitor the value (count) returned by the sensor. Select the Reset option to set the sensor count back to zero.

In the Compare section, select the motor's spin direction (Forward or Reverse) to monitor. Select Degrees or Rotations from the bottom drop-down menu, and enter a numeric value in the text box. You must also decide whether the sensor will monitor for a value less than or greater than the configured value by selecting the option in the other drop-down menu (using the Yes/No data plug, you can test for a True or False logic response based on the settings you have configured in the panel).

RIS Rotation Sensor

The RIS Rotation sensor's configuration panel is shown in Figure 9-10.

Figure 9-10. *The RIS Rotation sensor's configuration panel*

In the Port section, select the port where the RIS Rotation sensor has been connected. The default port for the Rotation sensor is Port 2.

In the Action section, you should select the Read option if you want the built-in rotation sensor to monitor the value (count) returned by the sensor. Select the Reset option to set the sensor count back to zero.

In the Compare section, select the motor's spin direction (Forward or Reverse) to monitor. Enter a numeric value in the text box for the number of ticks you wish to monitor; there are 16 ticks in 1 rotation. You must also decide whether the sensor will monitor for a value less than or greater than the configured value by selecting the option in the other drop-down menu.

RIS Temperature Sensor

The RIS Temperature sensor's configuration panel is shown in Figure 9-11.

Figure 9-11. *The RIS Temperature sensor's configuration panel*

In the Port section, select the port where the RIS Temperature sensor has been connected. The default port for the Temperature sensor is Port 4.

In the Compare section, you must enter a numeric Temperature value in the text box or use the drag bar to set a value. The value for Celsius must be in the range of –20 (negative 20) to 70. The value for Fahrenheit must be in the range of –4 (negative 4) to 158. Select the less than option (<) or the greater than option (>) from the drop-down menu, *or* click on the left or right radio button to configure this option.

In the Show section, select either Fahrenheit or Celsius from the drop-down menu. The value ranges the sensor can monitor are determined by this selection.

Other Input Types

There are three other methods that can be used to provide feedback to your NXT robots. These include the NXT buttons, the NXT timers, and a message received using Bluetooth technology by the NXT Brick using a RECEIVE MESSAGE programming block. I'll cover the RECEIVE MESSAGE block (and its partner, the SEND MESSAGE block) in Chapter 25, so let me close this chapter with details on the NXT buttons and timers.

Your NXT Brick has four buttons on its front: Left, Right, Enter (orange), and Cancel. The Cancel button cannot be used as input; its function is simply to cancel a running program, or if you are navigating around the on-screen LCD tools, it can be used to move back to a previous screen. That leaves the Left, Right, and Enter buttons—any program you create can use these three buttons to provide input.

Figure 9-12 shows the configuration panel for the NXT BUTTONS block.

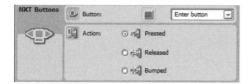

Figure 9-12. *The NXT buttons are configured here.*

In the Button section, select the button (Enter, Left, or Right) from the drop-down menu. The default selection is the Enter button.

In the Action section, select Pressed, Released, or Bumped. These work just like the Touch sensor, by the way.

The NXT Brick also has three built-in Timers. These timers begin counting the moment you press the Enter button to begin running a program. Figure 9-13 shows the TIMER block configuration panel.

Figure 9-13. *The NXT Timer configuration panel*

In the Timer section, select 1, 2, or 3 from the drop-down menu to select the timer you wish to use. The default selection is Timer 1.

In the Action section, select the Read option to obtain the current value of the timer. If you select Reset, the timer will be reset to zero when this block is executed.

The Compare section allows you to specify a value (in seconds) as a trigger that can be tested. Select either the greater than option or the less than option from the drop-down menu, and the TIMER block can now be used to provide a True/False Logic data type response. For example, if you configure the TIMER block for greater than 10 seconds for Timer 1, the Logic data plug will provide a False response until Timer 1 exceeds 10 seconds. After that, the data plug will provide a True response.

Using the Blocks

This chapter only showed you how to configure these blocks using the configuration panel. The real power comes with using these in conjunction with other blocks such as the LOOP, WAIT, and SWITCH blocks.

Chapter 11 will show you how to use the LOOP block to repeat certain tasks. When using a LOOP block, you can have the block *loop* forever, that is, performing the tasks over and over again until you cancel the program. Your other option is to configure the LOOP block to stop looping when a certain condition is met, for example, if the Light sensor detects a light level below 20, the Sound sensor detects a noise over level 80, or maybe a motor spins more than 20 degrees (Rotation sensor).

It's the same with the WAIT and SWITCH blocks. Both of these blocks will allow you to use what you've learned in this chapter to give your robots decision-making power.

So, read on—the WAIT block is up next in Chapter 10.

CHAPTER 10

Wait for It!

One of the most useful things your robots will be doing is waiting. Yep, you heard me right—waiting. Don't believe me? Okay, think about it this way:

- SPOT is moving toward a black line, *waiting* for the Light sensor to detect the line.

- SPOT is preparing to throw a ball at a target, *waiting* for the Touch sensor to be pressed and released.

- SPOT is rolling towards the wall, *waiting* for the Ultrasonic sensor to detect the wall.

- SPOT is sitting on the start line, *waiting* for the Sound sensor to hear me yell, "Go!"

Are you beginning to see that waiting is an important part of a robot's program? Your robots will probably *always* be waiting for something to happen. It may be as simple as waiting for you to press the Enter button on the Brick or something similar to the preceding examples. All this waiting is accomplished using the WAIT block, so keep reading to figure out how to program your bots to "wait for it!"

The WAIT Block

When discussing the WAIT block, you need to understand one important concept: The WAIT block will *stop waiting when specific conditions are met.*

It doesn't matter if you are using the Sound sensor, Touch sensor, Ultrasonic sensor, Light sensor, or a simple time limit. When you use a WAIT block, you must tell the WAIT block what conditions must be met before the waiting ends.

So, to show you how this works, let me give SPOT some more pseudo-code:

Me: SPOT, keep moving forward until something happens.

Vague, isn't it? What does "something happens" mean? Well, it can be anything:

- Until 5 seconds have passed

- Until the Sound sensor detects a loud noise

- Until the Ultrasonic sensor detects something 8 inches in front of it

Do you get the idea? I want SPOT to keep moving forward until a special condition is met. And with NXT-G, that condition can occur using a sensor, a timer, an NXT button, or a time limit. I'm going to go over each of these individually, so you'll see how the conditions are configured. To demonstrate the different conditions, I'm going to have you first create an extremely simple program for SPOT (or your own bot).

Open the NXT-G software, and start a new program. Drop a MOVE block on the workspace, and configure it to spin motors B and C forward with an Unlimited Duration and a Power setting of 50 (see Figure 10-1).

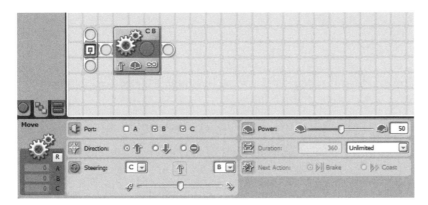

Figure 10-1. *A new NXT-G program for SPOT*

Now it's time to play around with different conditions that will end SPOT's forward movement. The WAIT block is our answer.

■**Note** When I discuss the WAIT block, I'm going to put another word in front of it to tell you how I will configure it. For example, a TIME WAIT block will use time as the condition. If I want to use the Sound sensor to end the wait, I'll use a SOUND SENSOR WAIT block. OK?

The WAIT blocks are found on the Common Palette. When you move your mouse pointer over the WAIT block, a fly-out menu appears with five options (see Figure 10-2).

Figure 10-2. *There are five WAIT blocks that can be selected.*

Let me start with the easiest to configure—the TIME WAIT block. Figure 10-3 shows the TIME WAIT block added and its configuration panel.

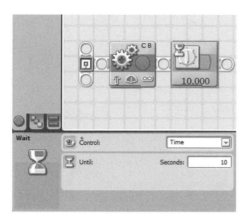

Figure 10-3. *The TIME WAIT block and configuration panel*

There are two items that can be configured on the TIME WAIT block. The first is a drop-down menu in the Control section. If you click this, you'll see that the WAIT block can be set to Sensor or Time. Don't change it yet, but be aware that by selecting Sensor you can change the TIME WAIT block to a SENSOR WAIT block. The Control section also gives you a couple of hidden WAIT blocks that I'll cover later in this chapter.

The other option in the TIME WAIT block that can be configured is the Until section. You'll notice that it expects you to enter a number in the text box for the number of seconds you wish for the WAIT block to . . . wait.

Figure 10-3 shows that I've configured the TIME WAIT block for 10 seconds. Go ahead and save the program, upload it to your bot, and then run it. What happens?

Did the motors run for 10 seconds and then stop? If not, check to make sure you configured the TIME WAIT block for 10 seconds; that's the most likely problem.

Well, that's it for the TIME WAIT sensor. Now let's take a look at the SENSOR WAIT blocks.

For the remaining WAIT blocks, I'm going to cover the configuration panels and the options available. I highly encourage you to practice these with the program you've just created: replace the TIME WAIT block with each of the WAIT blocks discussed in the following sections. Configure each WAIT block and play around with it; upload each to your bot, and see how it works.

To get started, let me give you a shortcut for changing the type of the WAIT block. Go back to your original program with the MOVE block and the TIME WAIT block (shown in Figure 10-3). Click the TIME WAIT block to access the configuration panel. Click the Control section's drop-down menu, and choose Sensor instead of Time. When you change to Sensor, you now have a new configuration panel section (called Sensor) with another drop-down menu. Click the drop-down menu, and take a look at your options (shown in Figure 10-4).

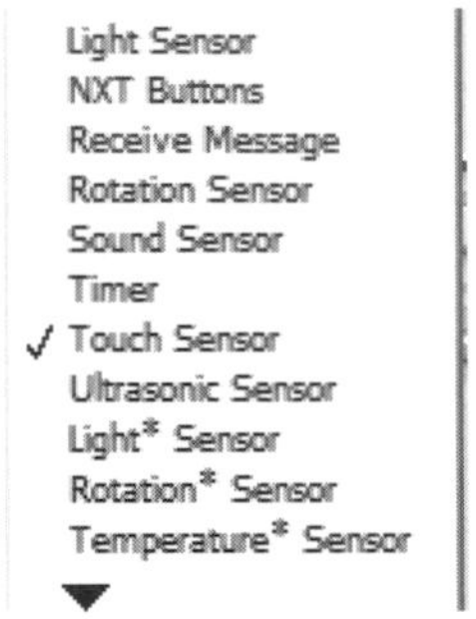

Light Sensor
NXT Buttons
Receive Message
Rotation Sensor
Sound Sensor
Timer
✓ Touch Sensor
Ultrasonic Sensor
Light* Sensor
Rotation* Sensor
Temperature* Sensor
▼

Figure 10-4. *The options available to you in the Sensor section drop-down menu*

The options provided include Light Sensor, NXT Buttons, Receive Message, Rotation Sensor, Sound Sensor, Timer, Touch Sensor, and Ultrasonic Sensor. The small triangle at the bottom indicates there are more sensors available, so click it to see them all. I'm going to cover each of these *except* for the Receive Message option; I'll cover the SEND MESSAGE and RECEIVE MESSAGE blocks in Chapter 25. So follow along as I show you each of these options and its corresponding configuration panel. Refer to Chapter 9 for details on the configuration panels for the sensors, NXT buttons, and timers.

The LIGHT SENSOR WAIT Block

Figure 10-5 shows the LIGHT SENSOR WAIT block and its configuration panel.

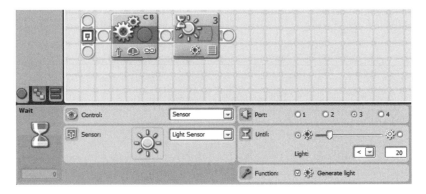

Figure 10-5. *The LIGHT SENSOR WAIT block and configuration panel*

In this example, the WAIT block has been configured to wait until the Light sensor detects a light level less than 20. When this occurs, the motors will stop spinning, and SPOT will stop moving forward.

The NXT BUTTONS WAIT Block

Figure 10-6 shows the NXT BUTTONS WAIT block and its configuration panel.

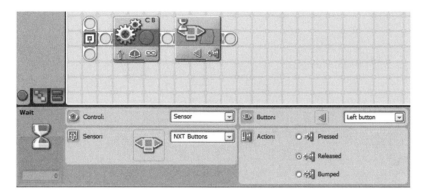

Figure 10-6. *The NXT BUTTONS WAIT block and configuration panel*

In this example, the WAIT block has been configured to wait until the Left button has been released. When this occurs, the motors will stop spinning, and SPOT will stop moving forward.

The ROTATION SENSOR WAIT Block

Figure 10-7 shows the ROTATION SENSOR WAIT block and its configuration panel.

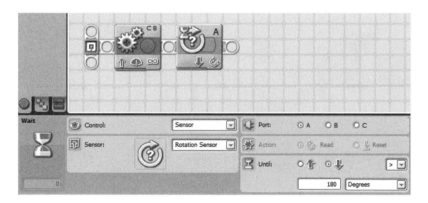

Figure 10-7. *The ROTATION SENSOR WAIT block and configuration panel*

In this example, the WAIT block has been configured to wait until motor A has spun in the Reverse direction for 180 degrees or more. When this occurs, motors B and C will stop spinning, and SPOT will stop moving forward.

The SOUND SENSOR WAIT Block

Figure 10-8 shows the SOUND SENSOR WAIT block and its configuration panel.

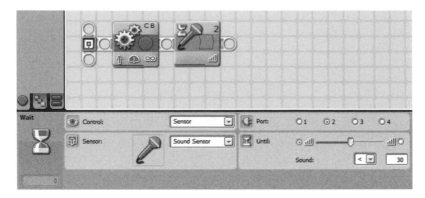

Figure 10-8. *The SOUND SENSOR WAIT block and configuration panel*

In this example, the WAIT block has been configured to wait until the Sound sensor detects a sound level below 30. When this occurs, motors B and C will stop spinning, and SPOT will stop moving forward.

The TIMER WAIT Block

Figure 10-9 shows the TIMER WAIT block and its configuration panel.

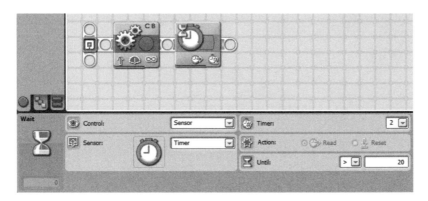

Figure 10-9. *The TIMER WAIT block and configuration panel*

In this example, the WAIT block has been configured to wait until Timer 2 exceeds 20 seconds. All timers start counting immediately when you run a program. So once you press the orange Enter button on the NXT Brick to run a program, this WAIT block will wait until the value read from Timer 2 equals 20 before the program continues. When this occurs, the motors will stop spinning, and SPOT will stop moving forward.

Later, you'll learn how to reset the timers, but for now, you just need to know that there are three timers—Timer 1, Timer 2, and Timer 3—and all start counting when a program starts.

The TOUCH SENSOR WAIT Block

Figure 10-10 shows the TOUCH SENSOR WAIT block and its configuration panel.

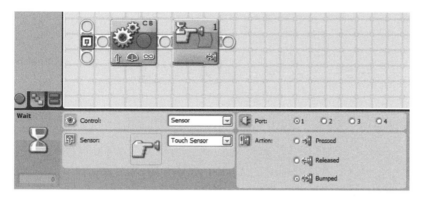

Figure 10-10. *The TOUCH SENSOR WAIT block and configuration panel*

In this example, the WAIT block has been configured to wait until the Touch sensor button has been Bumped (pressed and released quickly). When this occurs, motors B and C will stop spinning, and SPOT will stop moving forward.

The ULTRASONIC SENSOR WAIT Block

Figure 10-11 shows the ULTRASONIC SENSOR WAIT block and its configuration panel.

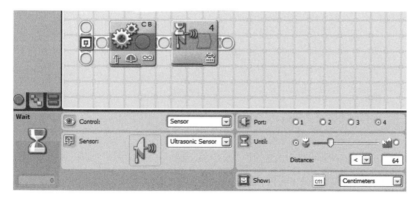

Figure 10-11. *The ULTRASONIC SENSOR WAIT block and configuration panel*

In this example, the WAIT block has been configured to wait until the Ultrasonic sensor detects an object (or obstacle) less than 25 centimeters in front of it. When this occurs, motors B and C will stop spinning, and SPOT will stop moving forward.

And that's it! Now you can configure your robots to wait for a variety of different conditions. You know how to use the sensors, the built-in timers, and the NXT buttons to trigger a WAIT block to stop waiting.

Now, let me ask you a question. You know how to make your robot wait and wait and wait—but do you know how to make your robot do something else over and over again? To do this, you'll use something called a LOOP block. I'll show you how it works in Chapter 11.

CHAPTER 11

■■■

Round and Round

At this point in the book, we're almost finished with the blocks in the Common Palette. Throughout the remainder of the book, I'll be introducing you to blocks and concepts that will allow you to build more complex programs than simply telling your bots to move forward, backward, or in a circle.

Now, I'd like to take a short break to introduce you to another concept. I'll make this one fun too, I promise. Then, I'll show you a new NXT-G programming block that you'll really like.

Do It Again and Again and Again . . .

Let's go back to our friendly bot, SPOT. Once again, let's just pretend that he's got a pair of ears and can understand verbal commands. I'm going to give him a set of unusual commands:

Me: SPOT, I want you to move forward six rotations, stop, and turn right.

[SPOT moves forward six rotations, stops, and turns right.]

Me: SPOT, move forward six rotations, stop, and turn right.

[SPOT moves forward six rotations, stops, and turns right.]

Me: SPOT, move forward six rotations, stop, and turn right.

[SPOT moves forward six rotations, stops, and turns right.]

Me: SPOT, move forward six rotations, stop, and turn right.

[SPOT moves forward six rotations, stops, and turns right.]

Now, where is SPOT? That's right—he's back where he started. The path he followed was square-shaped, and he's once again waiting for my instructions.

If you were to create an NXT-G program for SPOT to make this square, you'd simply place eight MOVE blocks on the workspace (as shown in Figure 11-1) and configure each MOVE block with the same two settings, right? One MOVE block will spin motors B and C for six rotations and the next MOVE block will have SPOT make a right turn. I then repeat this pattern three more times for a total of eight MOVE blocks.

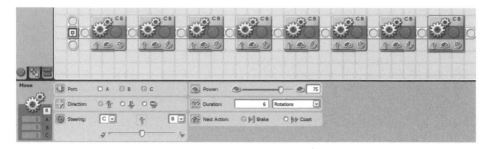

Figure 11-1. *NXT-G program for SPOT to follow a square-shaped path*

Well, it would work. But it seems like a *lot* of work just to make SPOT drive around in a square and return to his starting position. Is there a better way?

Let's see if we can improve the pseudo-code a bit:

Me: SPOT, I want you to move forward six rotations, stop, and turn right.

[SPOT moves forward six rotations, stops, and turns right.]

Me: SPOT, I want you to repeat my first set of instructions three more times.

[SPOT moves forward six rotations, stops, and turns right.]

[SPOT moves forward six rotations, stops, and turns right.]

[SPOT moves forward six rotations, stops, and turns right.]

Much better! I only had to tell him the instructions one time and ask him to do them again three more times. It takes just as long for SPOT to perform the movements, but I get to save my voice a bit!

In the pseudo-code, I gave SPOT commands, and I set a condition. You should be able to find the commands for SPOT: move, stop, turn right. But what is a condition? A *condition* is simply a rule your robot (SPOT) must follow. So my rule for SPOT is "Repeat my first set of instructions three more times." I could have told him to repeat it twice or 60 times; it doesn't matter as long as SPOT knows the rule and follows it.

Instead of telling him to repeat it three times, could I have used a different condition? Sure, here are some examples:

Me: SPOT, I want you to repeat my first set of instructions until your Touch sensor is triggered.

Me: SPOT, I want you to repeat my first set of instructions until your internal timer goes over 45 seconds.

Me: SPOT, I want you to repeat my first set of instructions forever.

Another way to look at it is that I've given SPOT instructions to do over and over and *over*—until something else happens. It could be that the Touch sensor is pressed or the Sound sensor detects a noise or the time reaches *infinity* (but trust me, SPOT's batteries won't last that long; eventually he'll stop)!

If SPOT keeps doing something over and over again, someone might say, "That robot is loopy!" And that's exactly right—he's *looping*.

What is a loop? In real life, a loop could be a road or a piece of string—no matter how large it is, if you follow its path, you'll eventually come back to your starting position. A programming loop is very similar. It just circles back on itself, either forever or until you program an *escape* from the loop.

And it just so happens that the NXT-G software has a block just for this special occasion—the LOOP block (see Figure 11-2).

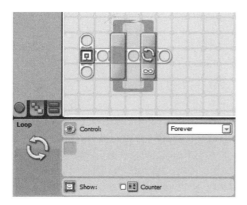

Figure 11-2. *A new NXT-G program for SPOT to follow a square-shaped path*

The LOOP block, by itself, is very boring. By default, it is set to loop *forever;* you can see this in the Control section of the LOOP block's configuration panel.

Right now, any block that I drop inside the LOOP block will keep repeating, over and over. Let me give you an example.

■**Note** When dropping a block inside a LOOP block, continue to hold down the mouse button and move the new block inside the LOOP block until the LOOP block expands.

I'm going to place a MOVE block inside the LOOP block. This MOVE block will be configured to spin the motors in Ports B and C for 1 Rotation (see Figure 11-3).

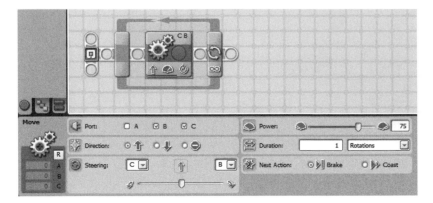

Figure 11-3. *A simple MOVE block inside a LOOP block*

I then save the program, upload it to SPOT, and run it. SPOT moves forward one rotation, and then there's a slight pause. Next, SPOT moves forward one more rotation, and there's another pause. This continues until I get tired of watching him, and I cancel the program.

The pause is occurring when the MOVE block finishes its action and the LOOP block checks its condition (this happens very quickly). Remember, the condition is a rule that the bot must follow. The rule for this program is for the LOOP to continue forever, so it runs again and again and again—you get the picture. That explains the short pause between rotations of SPOT's motors.

Now let's change the condition. How would we tell SPOT to run the MOVE block four times?

Take a look at the LOOP block's configuration panel. The Control section has a drop-down menu. Go ahead and click it, and you'll see some options (shown in Figure 11-4).

Figure 11-4. *The Control section of the LOOP block*

The options are Forever, Sensor, Time, Count, and Logic. Let me start with one of the easiest of the bunch: Time. Select Time from the drop-down menu in the Control section, and the configuration panel will change (see Figure 11-5).

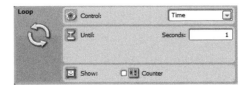

Figure 11-5. *The Control section of the LOOP block configured for Time*

When you select Time as the Control, you have access to two other sections. The Until section is where you'll enter a time (in seconds) in the text box. This is the amount of time that any programming blocks *inside* the LOOP block will run. Earlier I mentioned that a loop will cycle forever until you program an *escape*. Well, by setting this time limit, you've provided that escape from the loop. And that escape goes by another term—loop break.

A *loop break* occurs when the loop stops. After the loop break, your program will continue with the next programming block, or it will stop if the LOOP block is the last block in your program. Easy, isn't it? The loop can break if you cancel the program, but it can also be configured to break when a specific condition is met. In one of my earlier examples, I told SPOT to stop when the Touch sensor was bumped. The Touch sensor will break the LOOP block.

I need to make one important point: if there are multiple blocks inside the LOOP block, they will *all* complete before the LOOP block breaks. So if you configure your LOOP block to run for 25 seconds and the blocks inside take 40 seconds to finish, the 25-second time limit will expire before the internal blocks are finished, so the LOOP block will not loop again.

The other section, Show, has one option: you can either enable or disable the counter. Every time the LOOP block loops, the counter increases by one. If the box is checked, the LOOP block will provide a small data plug (see Figure 11-6). I covered data hubs and data plugs in Chapter 7, but what you need to know about this option is that you can use the data plug to provide an output Number data type. This Number value is the number of loops the LOOP block has performed.

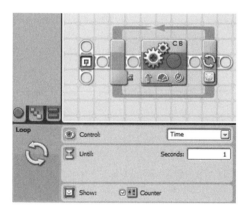

Figure 11-6. *If you select the Show option, a small data plug becomes available.*

Another easy option is the Forever setting shown in Figure 11-7.

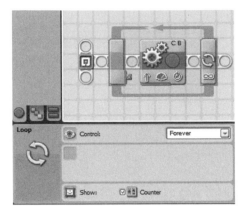

Figure 11-7. *A LOOP block set to Forever*

When you configure a LOOP block to run Forever, that's exactly what will happen: any blocks inside the loop will run over and over again until you cancel the program or the batteries give out.

Now click the drop-down menu in the Control section, and select Sensor; next, click the drop-down menu in the Sensor section to see the drop-down menu shown in Figure 11-8.

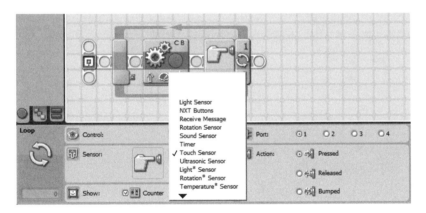

Figure 11-8. *A LOOP block configured for Sensor input*

As you can see, the Sensor section's drop-down menu offers the following options: Light Sensor, NXT Buttons, Receive Message, Rotation Sensor, Sound Sensor, Timer, Touch Sensor, and Ultrasonic Sensor. These were covered in Chapter 9 and are easy to use. What you are doing when you select one of these options is configuring the trigger that will break the loop.

For example, in Figure 11-9, I have selected the NXT Buttons options from the Sensor section drop-down menu.

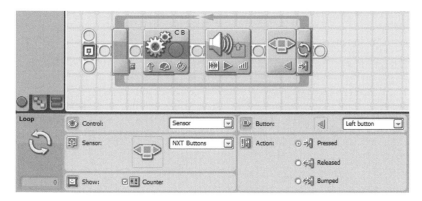

Figure 11-9. *A LOOP block configured to break when the Left button is pressed*

In this example, I have configured the loop to break when the Left button on the NXT Brick is pressed. Inside the loop, I have configured one MOVE block to move SPOT forward one rotation. I have also added a SOUND block that will play a short beep. Once the program is running, SPOT will move forward one rotation and beep, and he'll continue to do this until the Left button is pressed. (I'll have to chase him to press the Left button!)

Just keep in mind that when you choose an option from the Sensor section, you are configuring a condition that *must* be met before the LOOP block will break.

Your next possible option is to break the loop with a Count. Select Count from the dropdown menu in the Control section (see Figure 11-10).

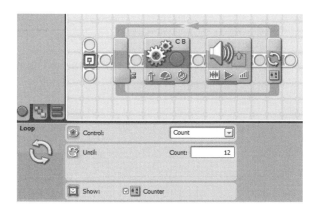

Figure 11-10. *A LOOP block configured to break using a Count*

When using the Count option, you must provide an integer value in the Until section's text box. You cannot use negative numbers, only zero and positive integers (1, 2, 3, and so on).

In Figure 11-10, I've configured the LOOP block to break when the Count reaches 12. When I run the program, SPOT will execute the first MOVE and SOUND blocks. When these are finished, Count goes from 0 to 1, and the loop starts again. The MOVE and SOUND blocks are executed again, and Count increases to 2. After the blocks have been executed a total of 12 times (Count = 12), the loop will break, and the program will end.

The last option available to break a loop is the Logic setting, shown in Figure 11-11.

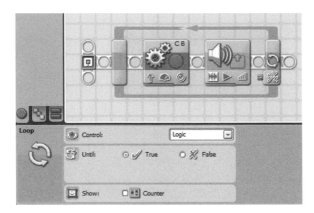

Figure 11-11. *A LOOP block configured to break using a Logic response*

In Figure 11-11, notice that when Logic is selected in the Control section drop-down menu, a small data plug appears on the LOOP block.

This data plug will only accept a Logic data wire as input. This means that the LOOP block will break when the Logic data type (True or False) you selected in the Until section is received. I'll show you an example using this option in the next section.

That's it for configuring an individual LOOP block. But there's one more thing I'd like to show you with the LOOP block: nested loops.

Nested Loops

To demonstrate this new concept, I'm going to create a simple program for SPOT that I'd like you to follow along and create yourself. First, let me explain what I want SPOT to do using pseudo-code:

> **Me**: SPOT, I want you to move forward along a circular path for 3.5 rotations and then use your speaker to beep! Do this two more times (for a total of three times), and then check to see if your Light sensor detects a Light level greater than 90. If the Light sensor is not triggered, repeat this entire process.

I can use a LOOP block to hold a MOVE block and a SOUND block that will repeat three times. This is shown in Figure 11-12.

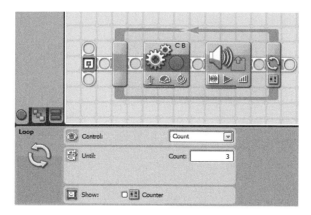

Figure 11-12. *This LOOP block contains a MOVE block and a SOUND block and will use a Count of 3.*

I've dropped a MOVE block and a SOUND block inside this LOOP block. In the Control section, you'll see that I've selected the Count option and set it to 3. The next thing I want to do is see if the Light sensor is triggered. I've added and configured the Light sensor in Figure 11-13.

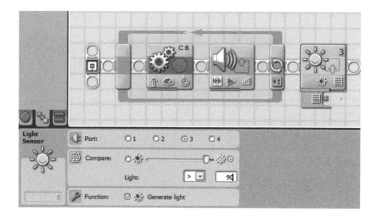

Figure 11-13. *The Light sensor is added to the program.*

But now I've got a problem. If you follow along with the program, you can see that the LOOP block will run three times: the MOVE and SOUND blocks inside it will execute three times and then the LOOP breaks. Then the Light sensor is tested. If the Light level is greater than 90, the program ends. But what if the Light level is less than 90? How do I make the program run again? One option is to simply have SPOT run the program again. I'll have to press the Enter button on the Brick to run the program again, but this will work. It will also be very annoying. There ought to be an easier way, and there is.

Take a look at Figure 11-14, and you'll notice that the entire program I just created is now *inside* another LOOP block.

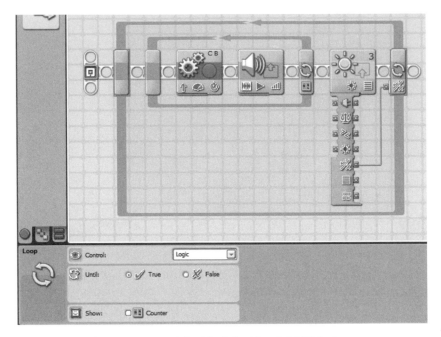

Figure 11-14. *There is now a LOOP block inside a LOOP block.*

This is called a *nested loop*, which just means a loop inside a loop. When the program runs, any blocks inside the outer LOOP block will run. First, the inner LOOP block will run three times (executing the MOVE and SOUND blocks inside it) and then break. Then the Light sensor will send a True/False Logic response to the outer LOOP block's data plug. If the Light sensor does not detect a light level greater than 90, the outer LOOP block will not break and will run whatever is inside it again.

Notice in Figure 11-14 that there is a data wire connecting the Light sensor to the outer LOOP block. In the Control section of the outer LOOP block, I've selected the Logic option and programmed it to wait Until it receives a True response from the Light sensor block. If the Light sensor block does not detect a light level greater than 90, the Yes/No data plug sends a False signal to the outer LOOP block, causing the outer LOOP block to loop again.

For my final example, Figure 11-15 shows a complicated situation. Can you determine what will happen?

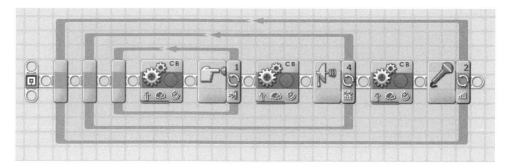

Figure 11-15. *LOOP blocks everywhere*

Yes, that is a loop inside a loop inside a loop—three LOOP blocks! If you examine this program carefully, you should be able to see what will happen when it is run.

First, the innermost LOOP block will begin to execute a MOVE block until the Touch sensor is triggered (in this case, bumped). Then the innermost LOOP block will break. Next, the middle LOOP block will begin executing a MOVE block until the Ultrasonic sensor is triggered. At that point, the middle LOOP block will break. Then the final, outer LOOP block will begin executing a MOVE block until the Sound sensor is triggered. Finally, when the Sound sensor is triggered, the outer LOOP block breaks, and the program ends.

The LOOP block is a very useful and powerful block; you should spend some time experimenting with all the different options. You'll use the LOOP block often when you want your robots to repeat certain blocks.

Now you know how to have your robot repeat certain actions such as turning left and moving forward 10 rotations. Up next in Chapter 12, I'm going to show you how to give your robots the ability to make choices: should SPOT turn left and move forward five rotations or turn right and move forward two rotations?

CHAPTER 12

■ ■ ■

Decisions, Decisions

This chapter covers the final block in the Common Palette. When you are finished with this chapter, you will have the ability to create some great little programs for your robots and give them the ability to move, talk, listen, bump, stop, wait, and a lot more.

Let's give your robots one more talent—the ability to make choices and select from multiple possible actions.

Left or Right? Door 1 or Door 2?

Let me give SPOT some pseudo-code for his next task:

Me: SPOT, I want you to move forward three rotations and stop. If your Light sensor detects a light level over 30, turn left. Otherwise, turn right.

At this point, you already know how to program SPOT with a MOVE block that moves him forward three rotations. But how do you take the light value from the Light sensor and use it to help SPOT make a decision about turning left or right?

The answer is easy; you'll use the SWITCH block shown in Figure 12-1.

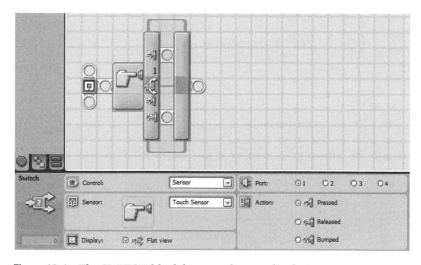

Figure 12-1. *The SWITCH block lets your bots make choices.*

The SWITCH block uses an input value to determine a path to take. This value can be a number, a bit of text, or a Logic value (True or False). And you're not just limited to two paths. You could configure a SWITCH block to handle the following pseudo-code:

Me: SPOT, pick a random number from 1 to 5.

Me: If the number is 1, turn left.

Me: If the number is 2, turn right.

Me: If the number is 3, spin 180 degrees.

Me: If the number is 4, spin 360 degrees.

Me: If the number is 5, keep moving forward.

In this example, I have SPOT pick a random number. This is done using the VARIABLE block that you'll learn about later in Chapter 18. But for now, let's just assume for the moment that SPOT can pick his own numbers. Now, since there are five potential numbers (1, 2, 3, 4, and 5), there are five potential actions that can be taken. Throughout the remainder of this chapter, I'm also going to use the term *path* instead of *action*, because the SWITCH block will allow your bots to choose from different paths available to them.

Depending on the path a robot selects, different actions will occur. One path can have your robot moving forward, checking its Ultrasonic sensor for an object in front. Selecting a different path might send the same robot in the reverse direction, waiting for its Touch sensor to be pressed and counting the number of rotations the motors spin. That's the great thing about the SWITCH block. Each potential path choice can have unique programming blocks that give your robots even more power. (And you can add another SWITCH block to a path, creating another set of paths for your robot to choose from!)

Now, before I show you how the SWITCH block works, I need to mention one special item in the SWITCH block's configuration panel. Take a look at Figure 12-2.

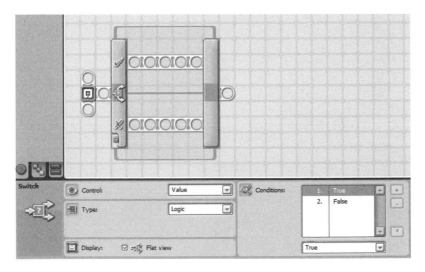

Figure 12-2. *Flat view for the SWITCH block*

When using the SWITCH block, you need to choose between Flat view and Tabbed view. When using Flat view, you need to leave the Flat view box checked (as shown in Figure 12-2). Flat view does have a limitation that you need to be aware of, however. When using it, you can program *only* two paths. Notice in Figure 12-2 that there are two paths: one labeled with a checkmark and the other with an "X". The checkmark path is also called the *default* path (more on this in a little bit).

Now, in Figure 12-3 I've unchecked the Flat view box, and you can now see that the SWITCH block has tabs along the top edge.

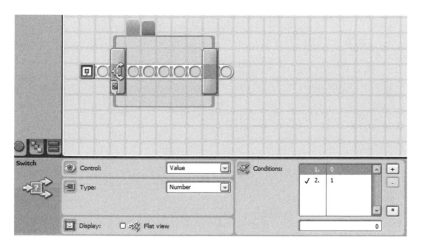

Figure 12-3. *Tabbed view for the SWITCH block*

With the Tabbed view, you must click a tab to see the programming blocks (if any) that have been placed inside it. This is a small price to pay for the ability to specify more than two options, however. Remember the earlier pseudo-code where SPOT picked a random number between 1 and 5? Figure 12-4 shows a SWITCH block with five tabs; each tab will now correspond to one of the potential actions I asked SPOT to perform.

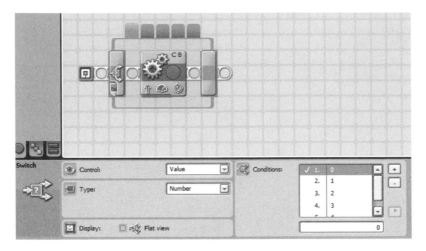

Figure 12-4. *This SWITCH block has five tabs for five different paths.*

Okay, now it's time to show you how to configure the SWITCH block, so you can use it to give your robot choices.

In Figure 12-5, I've placed a single SWITCH block that is using the Flat view. This means I only have two possible paths for my robot to take. The first path (with the checkmark) is on top and the second path (with the "X") is on the bottom.

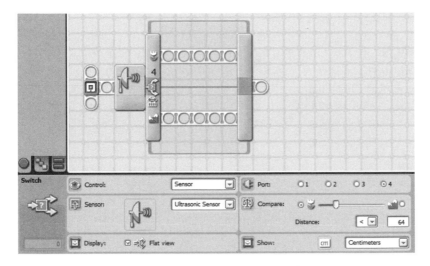

Figure 12-5. *This SWITCH block has two possible paths.*

This example also shows you the power of the SWITCH block. In the Control section, you have a pull-down menu that offers two options: Sensor and Value. Choosing the Sensor option will allow you to configure the SWITCH block to determine the correct path for your robot using the sensor and its trigger, which you select.

In this example, I've selected the Ultrasonic sensor. I've configured the Ultrasonic sensor to detect when an object or obstacle is detected less than 25 centimeters in front of the robot.

If this condition is met (True), the SWITCH block will execute any blocks found in the True path (the upper beam, with the checkmark). If the condition is not met (False), the SWITCH block executes any blocks found in the False path (the lower beam, with the "X" mark).

For the moment, let's assume that SPOT has his Ultrasonic sensor and Sound sensor mounted. I'm going to give SPOT the following pseudo-code:

Me: SPOT, when your Ultrasonic sensor detects an object less than 25 centimeters in front, turn left if your Sound sensor detects a sound level greater than 20.

I've already shown you how to configure the first SWITCH block to use the Ultrasonic sensor. So let's assume that SPOT's Ultrasonic sensor detects an object less than 25 centimeters in front of him. This means that any blocks on the upper beam (True path) will be executed. From the pseudo-code, we know that if the first condition is met, we want SPOT to turn left *only* if his Sound sensor detects a sound greater than 20. How will we do this? Simple—we'll use another SWITCH block!

First, I drop another SWITCH block on the top beam and configure it as shown in Figure 12-6.

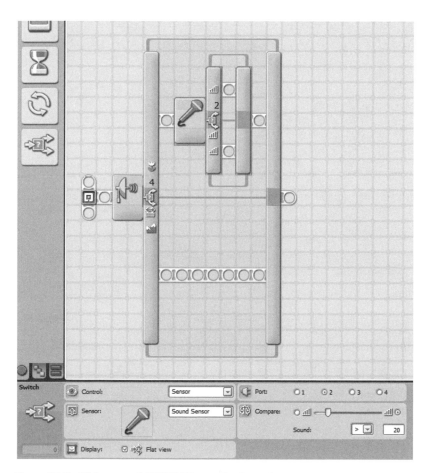

Figure 12-6. *This second SWITCH uses the Sound sensor.*

I configure the second SWITCH block to use the Sound sensor and to detect a sound greater than 20. If this happens, the True path (upper beam) in the second SWITCH block will execute any blocks found inside it. And that is where we'll place the MOVE block that allows SPOT to turn left (see Figure 12-7).

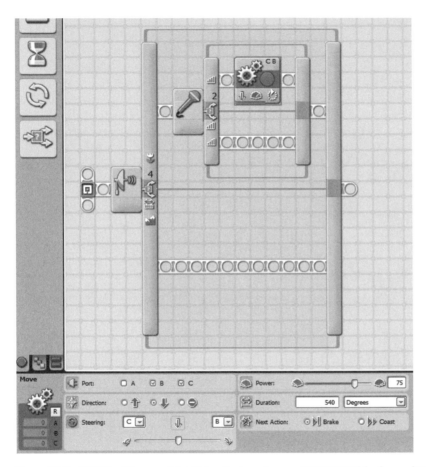

Figure 12-7. *SPOT will turn right if the first and second SWITCH block conditions are met.*

This is an example of embedded SWITCH blocks. You could keep going and place more SWITCH blocks inside other SWITCH blocks. This will give your robots some excellent decision-making control!

But what if you need to program your robot to test a greater number of conditions? Not all situations will have conditions that only have two options, right? So let's take another example for SPOT; look at Figure 12-8.

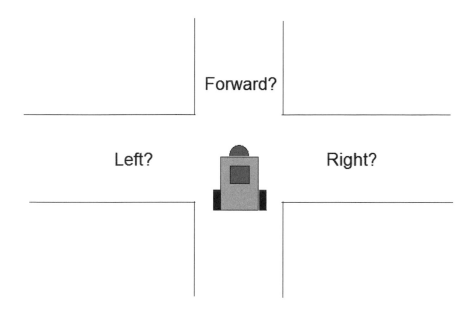

Figure 12-8. *SPOT has some decisions to make.*

Here's the pseudo-code:

Me: SPOT, when you come to the hallway intersection, pick a number from 1 to 3. If the number is 1, turn left. If the number is 2, turn right. And if the number is 3, move forward.

To do this bit of programming, recall that I told you you'll have to turn off the Flat view for a SWITCH block to use more than two conditions. That's the first requirement. The second requirement for configuring a SWITCH block for more than two paths is that the SWITCH block must be configured to use the Value option. This is found in the drop-down menu in the Control section and is shown in Figure 12-9.

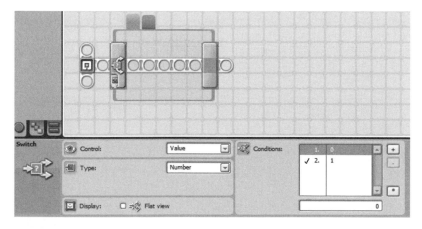

Figure 12-9. *Start with a SWITCH block with Flat view turned off and using a Value.*

The SWITCH block now has a small input data plug that will be used. This data plug can accept a Number data type, a Text data type, or a Logic data type, and you select the option from the drop-down menu in the Type section.

Using our pseudo-code, we can see that there are three possible conditions:

- Turn left if the number SPOT picks is 1.

- Turn right if the number SPOT picks is 2.

- If the number is 3, move forward.

For this example, I'm going to use the RANDOM block that is discussed in Chapter 14. For now, don't worry about how it works—just drag and drop a RANDOM block from the Complete Palette onto the beam, and place it in front of the SWITCH block as shown in Figure 12-10. (If you really want to know how the RANDOM block works, just jump ahead and read Chapter 14; I'll wait for you right here.)

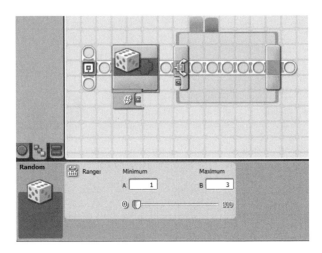

Figure 12-10. *A RANDOM block will generate a value of 1, 2, or 3.*

For the configuration panel of the RANDOM block, simply enter a value of 1 in the Minimum text field and a value of 3 in the Maximum text field, as shown in Figure 12-10.

Drag a data wire from the RANDOM block to the SWITCH block (see Figure 12-11).

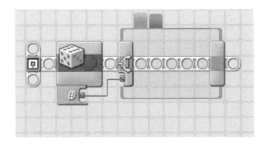

Figure 12-11. *Connect the RANDOM block to the SWITCH block with a data wire.*

Next, we need to configure the SWITCH block to accept more than two conditions. To do this, click the SWITCH block again (if it isn't already selected), and look at the configuration panel. On the left side of the configuration panel, you'll see the Conditions section (shown in Figure 12-12).

Figure 12-12. *The Conditions section of the SWITCH block*

Let me explain what you are looking at. This is a list consisting of path numbers. Each path number has a default value that the SWITCH block will check. In this example, you see the following:

1. 0

2. 1

The 1 and 2 on the left are the possible conditions, and these match the number of tabs you see along the top edge of the SWITCH block. The 0 and 1 values in the right column are the default Number values that the SWITCH block will use to pick a path. So, for example, if the Number value coming into the SWITCH block's data plug is 0, then the first condition will be selected, and any blocks found under the first tab will be executed.

Here's one more example to make sure you understand this concept. In Figure 12-13, I've got three tabs for the SWITCH block.

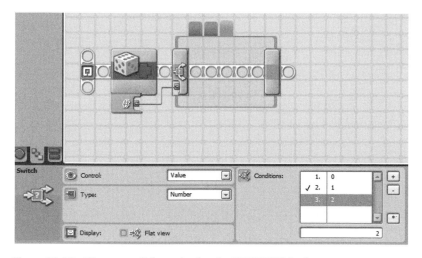

Figure 12-13. *Three possible paths for the SWITCH block*

Notice that there is now a new row in the Condition section:

1. 0

2. 1

3. 2

There are now three tabs on the SWITCH block. Tab 3 will have its blocks executed if the SWITCH block detects a Number value of 2.

Here we have a small problem: SPOT will pick only 1, 2, or 3. But the only options shown are 0, 1, and 2. How can we change this?

Easy—if you click one of the conditions, you can change its value in the text box just below the Condition section. First, click the condition whose value you want to change (see Figure 12-14).

Figure 12-14. *Click a Condition to change its value.*

Next, you must click on the small asterisk (*) button shown in Figure 12-15; this will place a checkmark next to the value of the condition that you want to change (see Figure 12-16).

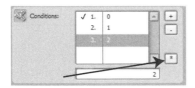

Figure 12-15. *Click the small asterisk (*) button to select a condition to change.*

Next, change the Number value in the text box just below the Condition section (see Figure 12-16).

Figure 12-16. *Change the Number value.*

In this example, I've changed the Number value for the third condition from 2 to 3. I'll perform these same actions for conditions 1 and 2, changing their values, respectively, to 1 and 2. This is shown in Figure 12-17.

■**Caution** Please be aware that you *cannot* have two or more conditions with the same Number value. This is because the SWITCH block would get confused and not know which path to take. Make sense? If condition 1 has a Number value of 1 and condition 2 has a Number value of 1, which path would the SWITCH block take if the RANDOM block sends a value of 1? Fortunately, the SWITCH block is smart and will not allow you to make this mistake.

Figure 12-17. *Three possible paths are now available to SPOT.*

And now I can drop in a collection of MOVE blocks that will allow SPOT to turn left, turn right, or move forward.

If SPOT picks 1, then he turns left. So, I'll click the first tab (see Figure 12-18) and drop in a MOVE block that will allow SPOT to turn left.

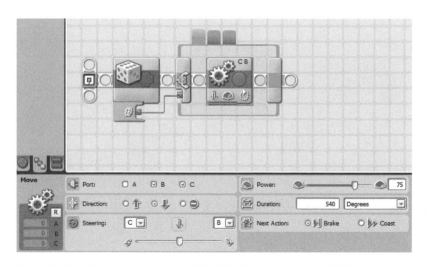

Figure 12-18. *The first tab has a MOVE block that executes if SPOT picks 1.*

I'll do the same thing for the second and third tabs. When the RANDOM block generates a number from 1 to 3, that number is passed to the SWITCH block. The SWITCH block takes this Number value and compares it to the values in its Condition section. If the RANDOM block sends a 3, the SWITCH blocks takes that value, notices that it equals the 3 in the third condition, and then executes any blocks found on the third tab. Easy!

One final warning, though—what happens if the RANDOM block goes crazy and sends a value of 4 to the SWITCH block? There is no condition that has a matching value of 4, so what will happen? Well, remember when you selected a condition and clicked the * button and a check-mark appeared next to the condition? That checkmark also specifies the *default condition.* Look back at Figure 12-16. The checkmark is next to the third tab. This means that if a value of 4 is provided by the RANDOM block and 4 isn't a possible value in the Condition section, the default path will be chosen. So the blocks in the third tab will execute for a value of 4, 5, 100, or any other number except for 1 and 2.

The SWITCH block is a very useful block for giving your robots some powerful decision-making skills. The SWITCH block can use Logic values (True or False), Numbers, Text, and sensors to determine which paths are chosen by your robot to execute. Keep this in mind when you need to give your robots the ability to make different decisions based on different types of input.

As your programming skills progress, you'll find the SWITCH block one of your favorite tools to use.

Next, we'll be looking into some specialty blocks.

CHAPTER 13

■■■

Stop It

This will be another short chapter. How much can one really say about a block that simply stops your program from running?

The STOP Block

The most important thing you need to know about the STOP block is this: if your robot encounters a STOP block at any point in the program, the robot will simply stop at that point with no further action (there is one exception and that is when you are using data wires—more on that later).

Your robot will always stop when it reaches the end of your program unless you have a LOOP block somewhere in the program that keeps the program running (or a LOOP block surrounding all other programming blocks, which means the program will run forever until you press the Cancel button or a STOP block is encountered somewhere in the inner workings of your program).

The STOP block is shown in Figure 13-1. Notice in its data hub that it only has one input data plug and one output data plug, which can use a Logic data type.

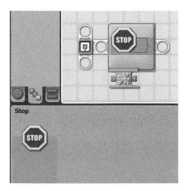

Figure 13-1. *The STOP block and its configuration panel*

As I mentioned earlier, the STOP block will immediately stop the program when the STOP block is reached *unless* a data wire is providing a False input (signal) to the STOP block's input data plug. Let's look at the example in Figure 13-2.

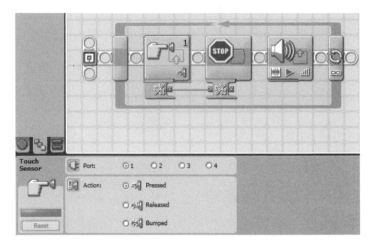

Figure 13-2. *A simple program using the STOP block*

In Figure 13-2, I've got a small program for SPOT. It's a LOOP block that contains a Touch sensor block, a STOP block, and a SOUND block. When the program is run, every time the LOOP block loops, SPOT will beep (using the SOUND block). This will continue until the Touch sensor is pressed. When the Touch sensor is pressed, a True response is sent (using the data wire) to the STOP block's input data plug. And the program will stop. As long as the Touch sensor is not pressed, the STOP block will continue to receive a False response from the Touch sensor and will not stop the program. Simple!

Now, what do you think would happen if I didn't connect a data wire between the Touch sensor and the STOP block, as shown in Figure 13-3?

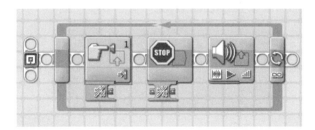

Figure 13-3. *Modifying the sample program's data wire completely changes the way it works.*

You can load the program and try it, but if you walk through the simple program visually I think you'll figure it out.

When the program runs, the LOOP block starts. The Touch sensor block runs, followed by the STOP block. Will the program execute the SOUND block? The answer is, "No." Remember my initial rule: the program will stop running when it executes a STOP block and will perform no further actions. This program will stop immediately and never execute the SOUND block (run the program to prove it to yourself).

You might be wondering when you would ever want to put a STOP block in the middle of a program. Well, one answer involves the SWITCH block. Recall that using the SWITCH block allows your robots to choose different action paths to take. One path might send your robot into some more complex programming behavior while the other path might be a simple STOP block. Take a look at Figure 13-4, which shows an example of this process.

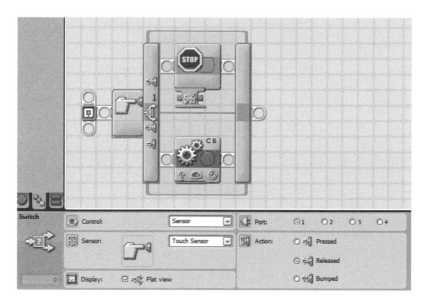

Figure 13-4. *A SWITCH block might need a STOP block to keep your robot safe.*

In this example, I've placed SPOT on a tall table. SPOT's Touch sensor is mounted facing downward on the table, so the button is pressed. If SPOT reaches the edge of the table, the Touch sensor button will no longer be pressed, right? (There's no table surface to continue to press against the button.)

Figure 13-4 shows a simple LOOP block that contains a SWITCH block. I've configured the SWITCH block to test whether the Touch sensor button is Released. If it is, the True path will be selected. If the button is still pressed, the False path will be selected. I want SPOT to stop immediately when the Touch sensor button is released, so I place a STOP block in the True path and a MOVE block in the False path. As long as the button is pressed, SPOT will keep moving forward. But for SPOT's safety, once the button is released (and he's reached the edge of the table), I want the program to immediately end. The trick to this program is placing the Touch sensor far out in front of SPOT, so he's still safely back from the edge when the button is released—try it!

The STOP block is extremely easy to use. As a testing tool, you can always place a STOP block in your program if you're testing a robot but don't want it to continue past a certain point in the program. For example, let's say you have a robot that performs three separate tasks, one after the other. Placing a STOP block after the programming blocks for the first task will allow you to run your program and test to make certain the program works for that task. If all is well, remove the STOP block and place another STOP block after the programming blocks for the second task. Now when you run the program, your robot will perform the steps for the first and second tasks but not for the third.

And now it's time to STOP this chapter and MOVE on to the NXT one; it's not a RANDOM chapter, but it does cover the RANDOM block. Sorry, I couldn't resist.

CHAPTER 14

■■■

Pick a Card, Any Card

Have you ever had someone perform a card trick and ask you to pick a card from the deck? There are 52 cards in a standard deck (the two jokers don't count), and if it's been properly shuffled, you should be able to pick a random card from the deck.

It's the same with rolling a pair of dice. Each die has the potential to roll a number from one to six. When you roll a normal pair of dice, the numbers that appear are random. The odds of rolling a 2 on one die are the same as rolling a 6; they all have the same likelihood of appearing. What allows this to occur is simple randomness.

Your robots also have the ability to generate random numbers. You might want to build a robot that can roll a virtual set of dice or maybe pick a number between 1 and 1,000. Read on to learn how to have your bots generate random numbers *and* display them on the LCD screen.

The RANDOM Block

Your bots can use the RANDOM block to generate numbers in a range that you define. The RANDOM block is found on the Complete Palette in the Data fly-out menu. Take a look at the block and its configuration panel in Figure 14-1.

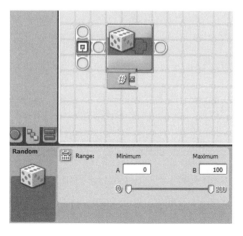

Figure 14-1. *The RANDOM block and its configuration panel*

The RANDOM block is another one of those blocks that is very simple to use. There are not a lot of options to configure, but what is there is important.

The first thing I want you to notice in the configuration panel is the Minimum and Maximum number fields in the Range section. In these boxes, you can type in the upper and lower values for the numbers you want the RANDOM block to generate. The Minimum value can never be less than 0, and the Maximum value can never be greater than 32,767.

There is one other method you can use for defining the Minimum and Maximum values. There are two small tabs on the Slider bar below the Minimum and Maximum values. You can drag the leftmost small tab to set the Minimum value. The rightmost small tab can be dragged to set the Maximum value.

■**Note** One thing you should be aware of is that the Slider bar can only be used for defining a range between 0 and 100. If you wish to use a Maximum value greater than 100, you need to type the number into the Maximum number field.

Now, let's do an example with SPOT using pseudo-code:

Me: SPOT, show a random number on your LCD screen between 20 and 80 until I press the left button.

To do this, I'll first drop a RANDOM block on the beam (see Figure 14-1). I've told SPOT that I want the Minimum value to be no less than 20, so I'll use the Slider bar to set the Minimum value (see Figure 14-2).

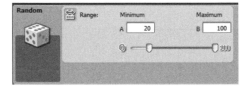

Figure 14-2. *The RANDOM block with the Minimum value set to 20*

Now, what if I had wanted the value to be between 20 and 80 but not include 20? Remember, the Minimum and Maximum values you define will be included in the possible numbers generated by the RANDOM block. So if I didn't want 20 to be a possible number, I would simply drag the Slider bar again to set the Minimum value to 21. By doing this, 21 would be a possibility, but 20 would be no longer allowed.

My final step is to set the Maximum value; I drag the Slider bar to set the Maximum value to 80 (see Figure 14-3).

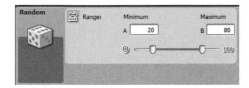

Figure 14-3. *The RANDOM block with the Maximum value set to 80*

Now all that's left to do is to have SPOT display the value on the LCD screen. To do this, I need to introduce you to another NXT-G programming block: NUMBER TO TEXT.

The NUMBER TO TEXT Block

The NUMBER TO TEXT block is also found on the Complete Palette in the Data fly-out menu. I'll drag and drop it after the RANDOM block, so you can see its configuration panel (shown in Figure 14-4).

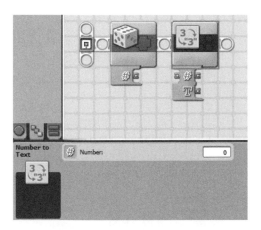

Figure 14-4. *The NUMBER TO TEXT block is for displaying numbers on the LCD screen.*

If you're wondering why the configuration panel is grayed out, it's because the NUMBER TO TEXT block requires the number it will display on the LCD screen to come into its single-input data plug. The number that is passed to this block is converted to text that can be displayed using the DISPLAY block.

So, let me go ahead and drag a wire from the output Number data plug on the RANDOM block into the input Number data plug on the NUMBER TO TEXT block. You can see this in Figure 14-5.

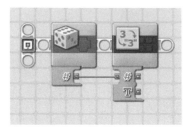

Figure 14-5. *Drag a wire from the RANDOM block to the NUMBER TO TEXT block.*

As you can tell from Figure 14-5, the text you want to display will come from the output data plug on the NUMBER TO TEXT block. I'll drop in a DISPLAY block and drag another wire from the output Text data plug on the NUMBER TO TEXT block into the input Text data plug on the DISPLAY block (see Figure 14-6). Remember to set the DISPLAY block to display Text, not Image or Drawing, in its configuration panel.

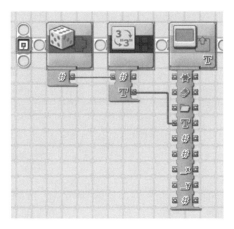

Figure 14-6. *Drag a wire from the NUMBER TO TEXT block to the DISPLAY block.*

Instead of using a TIME WAIT block to keep the text on screen as I've done with past examples, I'm going to use an NXT BUTTON WAIT block this time. The RANDOM number generated will stay on the LCD screen until I press the Left button.

To do this, I drop in an NXT BUTTON WAIT block and configure it as shown in Figure 14-7.

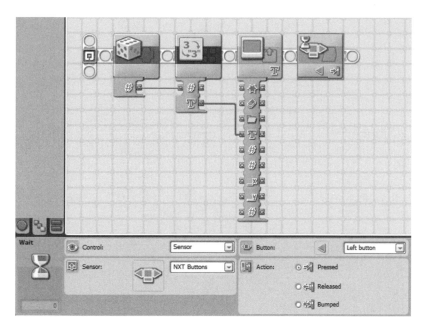

Figure 14-7. *The generated number will stay on the LCD screen until the left button is pressed.*

I've used a WAIT block with the Control section set to Sensor. In the Sensor section, I selected NXT Buttons from the drop-down menu. For the Button section, select Left button from the drop-down menu, and finally, in the Action section, I selected Pressed. By configuring the WAIT block this way, the random number will stay on the LCD screen until I press the left button on the NXT Brick. Then the program ends.

Not too difficult, huh?

One final thing I want to point out on the NUMBER TO TEXT block is the output Number data plug. This block will still allow you to keep and use the random number you generated in a Number format. You might need that random number later in the program. If so, you can drag a data wire out of the output Number data plug—it will still be a number and not changed to text.

So now you know how the RANDOM block is configured and used. If you want your robot to move randomly around the room, for example, you could configure a RANDOM block to generate a number between 1 and 4. Program your bot to go left if the number is 1, right if the number is 2, forward if the number is 3, and in reverse if the number is 4. By using a random number to control the bot's direction, you can give the bot some unpredictable behavior. Refer to Chapter 12's discussion of the SWITCH block for using conditions such as a random number to control movement.

Next, in Chapter 15, we'll look at the COMPARE block.

CHAPTER 15

■ ■ ■

Apples and Oranges

There's an old saying, "That's like comparing apples to oranges." What it means is that it's sometimes unfair to compare dissimilar objects. I said "sometimes," because at other times it's completely fair. Suppose I hand you one apple and one orange. Which one is heavier? Which one has a larger diameter? These aren't unfair questions, are they?

So sometimes you *can* compare apples to oranges! And when it comes to your robots, there's a way for your robots to compare things, too—not apples and oranges but numbers.

The COMPARE Block

Remember that we discussed the concept of Logic back in Chapter 8? True or False? (If you said False, you need to go back and read Chapter 8 again!)

Well, NXT-G comes with a programming block called the COMPARE block that relies on your understanding of Logic.

Suppose I ask you, "Is 5 greater than 3?" Your answer would be, "Yes." When you program, the same question is given to a computer or robot in the form of a statement, "5 is greater than 3." This statement, to your robot, is either True or False.

Similarly, if I ask you, "Is the Earth square-shaped?" you would answer, "No." A robot would not be asked this question, but instead told, "The Earth is square-shaped." And it would respond with False.

So, here's an important item to remember: robots respond to statements with True or False.

Before I show you the COMPARE block, let's create a test program for SPOT using pseudo-code:

Me: SPOT, I want you to create two random numbers between 1 and 9 (number A and number B), show them on the LCD screen, and tell me if A is greater than B.

To do this, we'll start by dropping two RANDOM blocks (see Chapter 14) on to the beam, as shown in Figure 15-1. I've configured both RANDOM blocks with identical settings, as shown in the configuration panel.

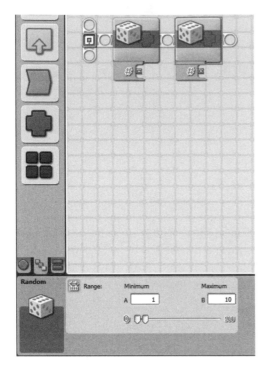

Figure 15-1. *Two RANDOM blocks will generate numbers for comparison.*

Next, I'll convert them to text using two NUMBER TO TEXT blocks (see Figure 15-2). Review Chapter 14 for information on the NUMBER TO TEXT block.

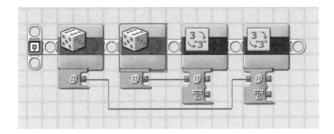

Figure 15-2. *Convert the random numbers to Text.*

And before we get to the Compare block, I'll use a TEXT block to create a statement in the form of "A greater than B," as shown in Figure 15-3.

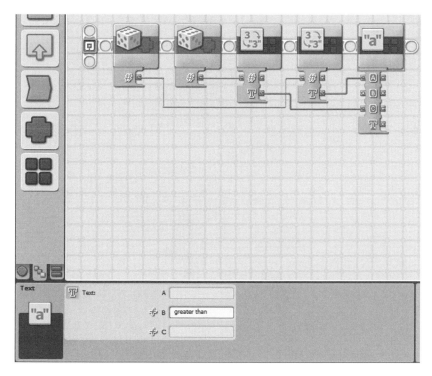

Figure 15-3. *Create a text statement to be displayed on the LCD screen.*

As you can see from Figure 15-3, the first RANDOM block number is used as input in the second NUMBER TO TEXT block (the fourth block from the left). The second RANDOM block number is used as input in the first NUMBER TO TEXT block (the third block from the left).

For the TEXT block, I have taken the first number (now converted to text) and used it as input to the A data plug. Also, I have taken the second number (now converted to text) and used it as input to the C data plug. I enter the words "greater than" in the B text box. This will create a single sentence (also called a *statement*): A greater than C (where A and C will be numbers between 1 and 9).

I now send the combined text to a DISPLAY block configured to display Text on Line 3 with position X=2 and Y=40 (see Figure 15-4).

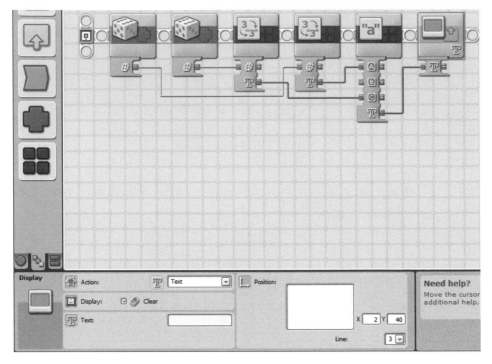

Figure 15-4. *The DISPLAY block will display a statement on the LCD screen.*

Now we're ready to see how the COMPARE block works. (Sorry it took so long to get here, but the COMPARE block by itself can't do anything—we need a good example with things to compare to see it in action.)

I'm going to break off a new beam to run in parallel. To do this, I hold down the Shift key and drag an extra beam, shown in Figure 15-5.

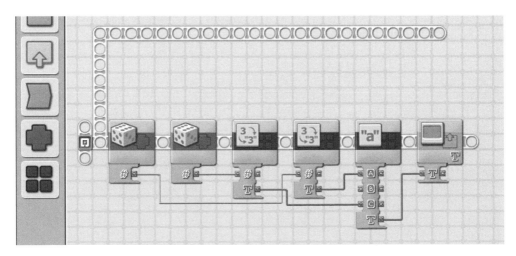

Figure 15-5. *An extra beam will be used to compare values.*

This parallel beam will let me compare value A to value B. Remember, I want to check the statement "A greater than B" and determine if it is True or False.

The first thing I need to do is drop the COMPARE block onto the new beam, as shown in Figure 15-6.

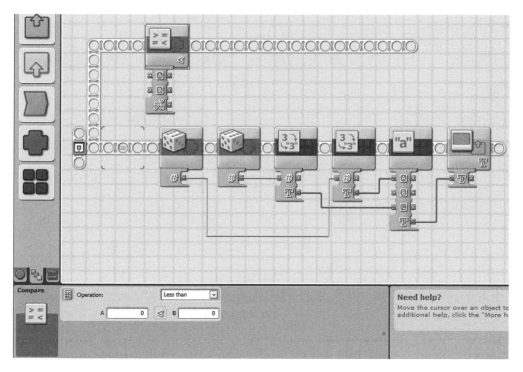

Figure 15-6. *The COMPARE block will check to see if value A is greater than value B.*

Notice in Figure 15-6 that the COMPARE block has two input data plugs. I'll take the original random numbers from the NUMBER TO TEXT blocks' output Number data plugs and drag data wires into the two COMPARE block input data plugs.

■**Note** Back in Chapter 14, I told you that the NUMBER TO TEXT block had an output Number data plug that could be used to keep the number in Number format and not Text format. You'll use this ability now to send these original random numbers into the COMPARE block.

Carefully drag a data wire out of the second NUMBER TO TEXT block (the fourth one from the left) and into the value A's input data plug. Do the same for the first NUMBER TO TEXT block (the third from the left). This configuration is shown in Figure 15-7.

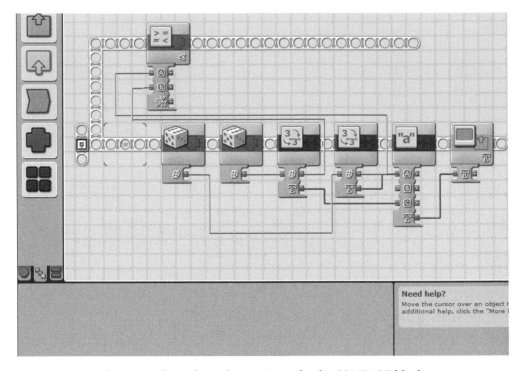

Figure 15-7. *Use the original number values as input for the COMPARE block.*

Now, click the COMPARE block to view its configuration panel (shown in Figure 15-8).

Figure 15-8. *The COMPARE block's configuration panel*

The COMPARE block's configuration panel has a drop-down menu in the Operation section. Click this drop-down, and you'll see three options: Less than, Greater than, and Equals.

If you choose the "Less than" option, the COMPARE block will evaluate the statement "A Less than B" and determine if it is True or False. If you choose the "Greater than" option, the COMPARE block will evaluate the statement "A Greater than B" and determine if it is True or False. And if you choose the Equals option, the statement "A Equals B" will be evaluated.

For my example, I choose the "Greater than" option, as shown in Figure 15-8. Now, my program will take the values for A and B and check to see if A is greater in value than B. The COMPARE block does this, and the answer will come from the output Result data plug.

If we go back to the pseudo-code, we'll see that I wanted True or False to be displayed on the LCD screen along with the original statement "A greater than B." To do this, I'm going to use the SWITCH block I covered in Chapter 12.

There are a bunch of items I need to configure for this to work. I drop a SWITCH block after the COMPARE block, and in the Display section, I uncheck the Flat view box (see Figure 15-9). In the Control section, I choose Value, and in the Type section, I choose Logic. I also drag a data wire out of the output Result data plug on the COMPARE block and connect it to the input data plug on the SWITCH block.

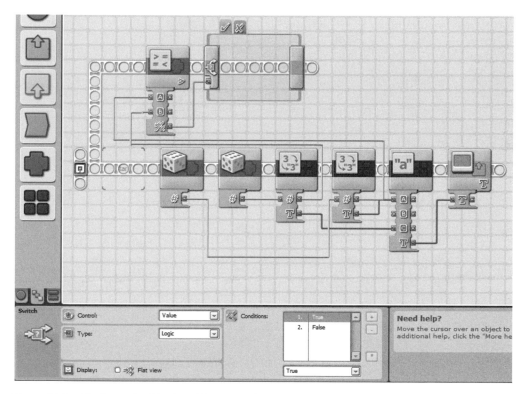

Figure 15-9. *The SWITCH block will help me display True or False on the screen.*

Next, I need to decide what will happen when the SWITCH block receives a True or a False signal from the COMPARE block. Let's start with the True tab; it's already selected in Figure 15-9.

I want to send the word "True" to the LCD display if the statement is True, so I'll drop in a TEXT block that will contain the word "True." This is shown in Figure 15-10.

In order for this text to appear on the LCD screen, I need to drop in another DISPLAY block on the original beam (see Figure 15-11). I drag a data wire out of the output Text data plug into the input Text data plug on this new DISPLAY block (I configured the block to display Text, and I also unchecked the Clear box).

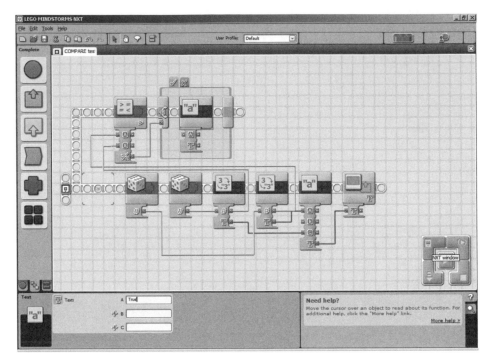

Figure 15-10. *This TEXT block contains the text "True".*

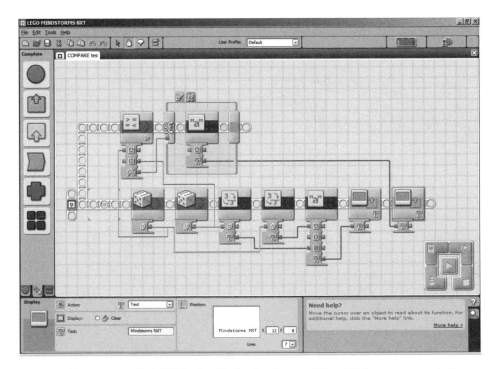

Figure 15-11. *A new DISPLAY block will display the text "True" if the statement is True.*

Now, to finish up this example, I click the other tab (the False tab) of the SWITCH block and drop a TEXT block inside, configured to hold the word "False." Just like the True tab, I drag a data wire out of the output Text data plug into the input Text data plug on a new, third DISPLAY block, as shown in Figure 15-12.

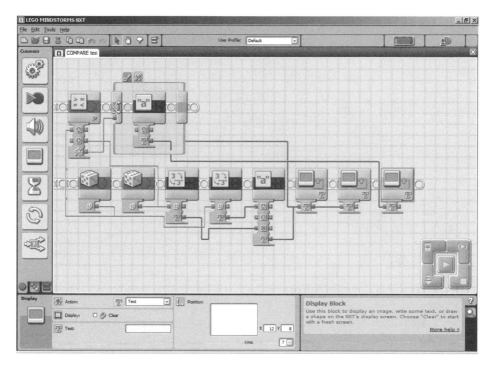

Figure 15-12. *The new DISPLAY block will display the text "False" if the statement is False.*

Finally, I drop in a NXT BUTTON WAIT block configured to wait for the left button to be pressed. This will give me time to view the results on the LCD screen (see Figure 15-13).

Let's walk through the program and see how it works. First, two RANDOM blocks generate two numbers, A and B. These numbers are converted to text (with the NUMBER TO TEXT blocks) and these "text numbers" are combined to create a text statement, "A greater than B," which is fed into a DISPLAY block.

After the random numbers are generated, these numbers are also fed into the COMPARE block, which takes the two numbers and looks to see if A is greater than B. If it is, the SWITCH statement executes the TEXT block in the True tab and displays the word "True" on the LCD screen. If A is not greater than B, the SWITCH statement executes the TEXT block in the False tab and displays the word "False" on the screen.

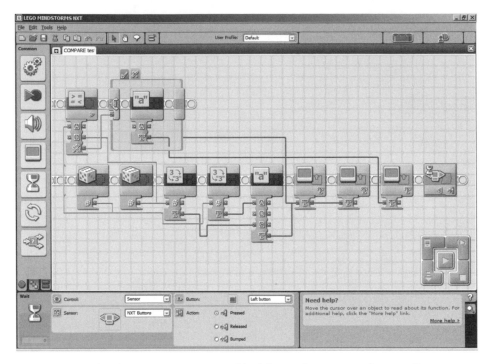

Figure 15-13. *A final NXT BUTTON WAIT block keeps the program from ending.*

I encourage you to create this program and test it yourself. You'll gain a better understanding of using wires, and you can tinker with it. Play around with changing the condition to "Less than" or Equals and see how the results change.

When you are finished, continue on to the next chapter, where I'll introduce you to the RANGE block.

CHAPTER 16

■ ■ ■

Inside or Out?

In the last chapter, you learned how to use the COMPARE block to test whether a value was less than, greater than, or equal to another value. The block compares the two numbers and determines whether the statement (A Less than B, A Greater than B, or A Equals B) was True or False.

Sometimes, however, you want to check to see if a value falls inside or outside a range of numbers: Is 28 inside the range 2 through 30? True. Is 50 outside the range 1 through 10? True.

NXT-G provides a block that allows you test the condition of a number (A) to determine whether it falls inside or outside the range of two other numbers (B and C). Here's how it works.

The RANGE Block

Just like the COMPARE block, the RANGE block uses the following rule: robots respond to statements with True or False.

The statements that a RANGE block will evaluate look like these:

- A is inside the range of numbers beginning with B and ending with C.

- A is outside the range of numbers beginning with B and ending with C.

That's it. The RANGE block evaluates the statement and returns a True or False response. Let's build a small program for SPOT that can use the RANGE block. As usual, we'll start with the pseudo-code.

Me: SPOT, I want you to create a random number between 1 and 100, show it on the LCD screen, and tell me if it is inside the range of 40 to 60.

To do this, we place one RANDOM block on to the beam and configure it as shown in Figure 16-1.

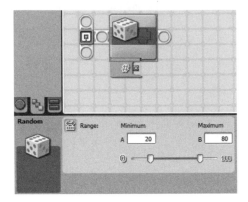

Figure 16-1. *A RANDOM block generates a number between 1 and 100.*

Next, I convert the number to text using a NUMBER TO TEXT block (see Figure 16-2).

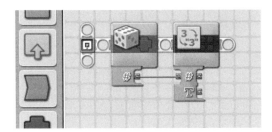

Figure 16-2. *Convert the random numbers to Text.*

Next, I'll add a TEXT block to create a statement in the form of "A between 40 and 60" as shown in Figure 16-3.

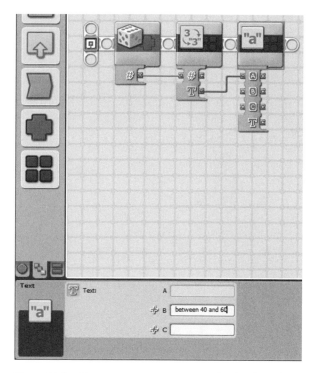

Figure 16-3. *Create a text statement to be displayed on the LCD screen.*

In Figure 16-3, the RANDOM block number is used as input to the NUMBER TO TEXT block. The TEXT block then takes this bit of text (A) and combines it with the statement "inside range."

In Figure 16-4, I use a data wire to send the text from the TEXT block to a DISPLAY block configured to display Text on Line 3 with position X=2 and Y=40 (see Figure 16-4).

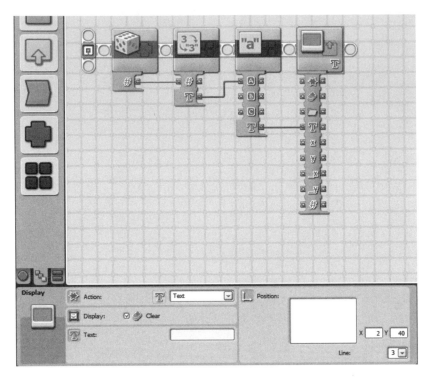

Figure 16-4. *The DISPLAY block will display "[number] inside range".*

I need to add one more DISPLAY block, so I can add the text "40 and 60" on Line 4 with position X=2 and Y=32 (see Figure 16-5). Remember to remove the check from the Clear box, so the text in the first DISPLAY box doesn't disappear!

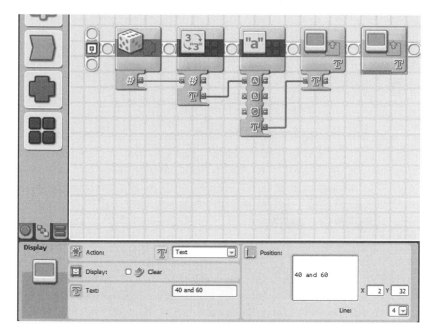

Figure 16-5. *This DISPLAY block puts "40 and 60" on the screen on the next line.*

And now it's time to use the RANGE block to evaluate the statement. I drop the RANGE block onto the beam as shown in Figure 16-6.

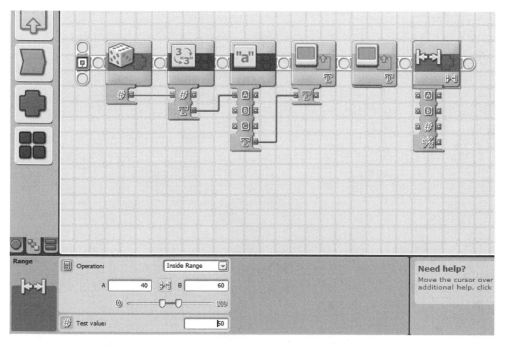

Figure 16-6. *The RANGE block will check to see if A is inside the range of 40 to 60.*

In Figure 16-6, you can see that I've selected Inside Range in the drop-down menu for the Operation section. I've also entered a value of 40 in the A field and 60 in the B field. I could have used the Slider bar to select the Lower Limit and Upper Limit for the range, but keep in mind that the Slider bar will only allow you to define a range between 0 and 100. If you need a larger range, you'll have to enter the values manually.

Note The other option in the drop-down menu is Outside Range. If I select this option, the statement will be True if the random number is outside the range of 40 to 60 and False if it is inside the range. Also notice that a Test Value can be entered in the Test Value field. You can use this if you do not have a number from an outside block (a RANDOM block, for example) to use as input. And finally, the Upper Limit and Lower Limit can also be provided to the RANGE block dynamically by using data wires to provide input (in Number format) to the Upper Limit data plug and the Lower Limit data plug.

My next step is to run a data wire into the RANGE block that contains the original random number. There are two ways to do this. The first is to drag a data wire out of the NUMBER TO TEXT block (remember that this block has an output data plug for the original Number). I used that method in Chapter 15 for the COMPARE block. Now I want to show you the other method.

If you click the output Number data plug on the RANDOM block, you can drag a data wire to the input Test Value data plug on the RANGE block. I've done this in Figure 16-7. Notice that the original data wire going into the NUMBER TO TEXT block now splits into two wires—one still goes in the NUMBER TO TEXT block, and the other goes into the RANGE block.

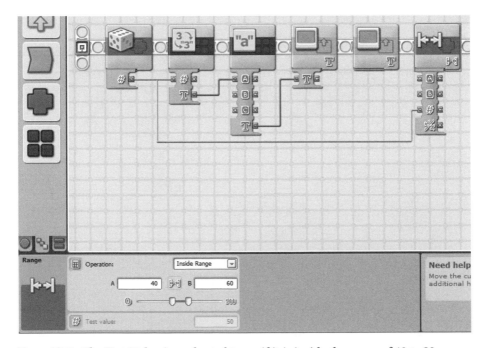

Figure 16-7. *The Test Value is evaluated to see if it is inside the range of 40 to 60.*

The pseudo-code tells SPOT to display on the LCD screen whether the statement "[number] inside range 40 and 60" is True or False. To do this, I've dropped a SWITCH block after the RANGE block. In the Display section, I uncheck the Flat view box; in the Control section, I choose Value, and in the Type section, I choose Logic. I also drag a data wire out of the output Result data plug on the RANGE block and connect it to the input data plug on the SWITCH block (see Figure 16-8).

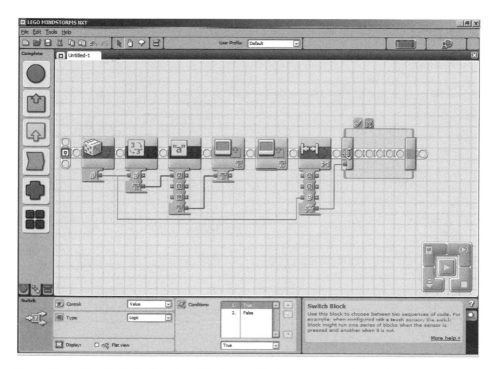

Figure 16-8. *The SWITCH block will help me display True or False on the screen.*

Now all that is left is for the LCD screen to display "True" or "False." This is simple enough: I'll drop one DISPLAY block in the True tab (see Figure 16-9) that puts the word "True" on the LCD screen on line 7. I'll drop another DISPLAY block in the False tab (see Figure 16-10) that puts the word "False" on the LCD screen on line 7 (remember to remove the check from the Clear box so text on the LCD screen doesn't get erased).

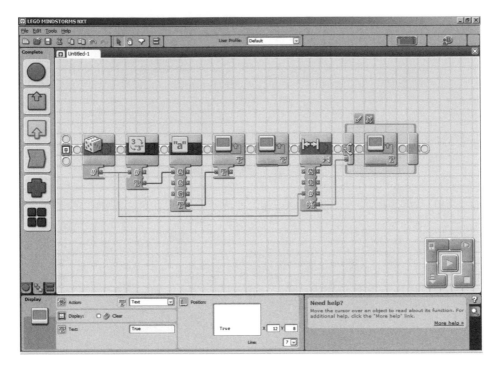

Figure 16-9. *This DISPLAY block puts the word "True" on the screen.*

Now, if the statement is evaluated as True, the SWITCH block will execute the DISPLAY block found in the True tab. And if the statement is evaluated as False, the SWITCH block will execute the other DISPLAY block found in the False tab.

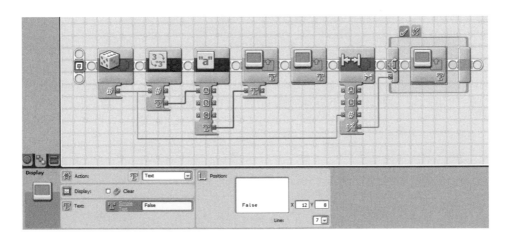

Figure 16-10. *This DISPLAY block puts the word "False" on the screen.*

Next, I'll drop in a NXT BUTTON WAIT block and configure it to wait for the left button to be pressed (see Figure 16-11). This will allow me time to view the results.

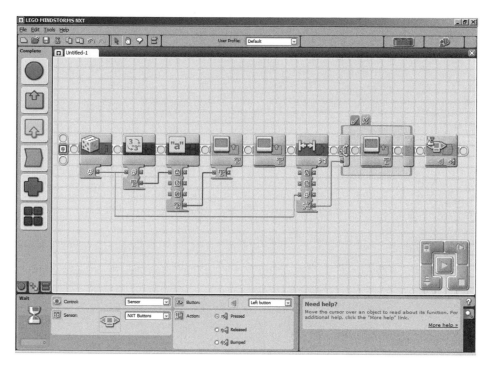

Figure 16-11. *The NXT BUTTON WAIT block gives me time to view the results.*

Play around with the program. Try the Outside Range option, and change the range of the RANDOM block. Experiment with the program until you have a solid understanding of how the RANGE block works.

When you're finished, continue on to Chapter 17, where I'll cover the LOGIC block.

CHAPTER 17

■■■

Yes? No? Maybe?

In Chapter 15, I introduced you to the COMPARE block, which takes two numbers, A and B, and examines them to determine if A is greater than, less than, or equal to B (depending on the option you select). The result of this comparison is then converted to a Logic data type (either True or False) that can be used as output using a data wire.

Well, in this chapter, I'm going to show you a block that is similar to the COMPARE block but not quite the same. Instead of comparing two numbers, this block will compare two Logic data type inputs and output the True/False Logic data type response.

The LOGIC Block

The Logic block (shown in Figure 17-1) is an interesting one.

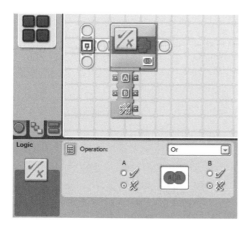

Figure 17-1. *The LOGIC block and its configuration panel*

Let me set up a scenario for SPOT that I think will help you understand how this block works. I've attached a Light sensor and a Sound sensor to SPOT. Here's my first bit of pseudo-code for SPOT to try out:

Me: SPOT, I want you to move forward three rotations if two conditions are True.

Me: The first condition is that the Light sensor detects a light level below 30.

Me: The second condition is that the Sound sensor detects a sound level below 20.

OK, what will happen here? Well, SPOT will check to see if his Light sensor detects a low light level in the room (< 30). He'll also check to see if his Sound sensor is detecting a quiet room (<20). Recall from our discussion of sensors that a sensor can return a True or False reply based on the conditions you have configured the sensor to detect.

Let's start our program by dropping a Light sensor block on the beam and configuring it as shown in the configuration panel in Figure 17-2.

Figure 17-2. *Configure the Light sensor as shown in the configuration panel.*

Next, we'll add a Sound sensor block and configure it as shown in Figure 17-3.

Figure 17-3. *Configure the Sound sensor as shown in the configuration panel.*

Now we have two sensors that will check the conditions of the light and sound in the room.

If we look back at our pseudo-code, SPOT will move forward *only* if both of the sensors are triggered. This means the Light sensor must receive a value less than 30 for the room's lighting level, and the Sound sensor must receive a value less than 20 for the room's sound level—both conditions *must* exist, or SPOT will not move forward.

What will happen if the room is bright and quiet? SPOT will *not* move.

What will happen if the room is dark and loud? SPOT will still not move.

What happens if the room is bright and loud? SPOT will get a headache. Just kidding—he still won't move.

So, how can SPOT quickly examine the lighting and sound conditions of the room and decide if he can move forward or not? Simple—he'll use the COMPARE block.

Go ahead and drop the COMPARE block on the beam, as shown in Figure 17-4.

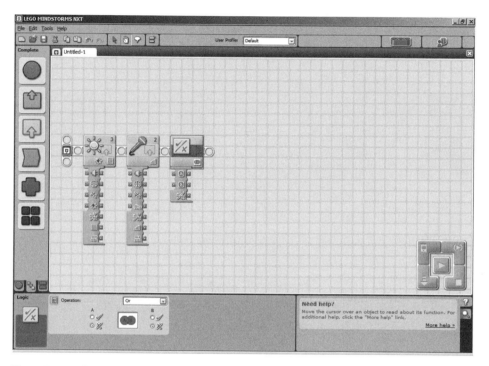

Figure 17-4. *The COMPARE block helps SPOT to examine the light and sound conditions.*

Take a look at the drop-down menu in the Operation section. The drop-down menu has four options: And, Or, Xor, and Not. For now, select the And option (I'll explain the other three options shortly).

Next, I want you to drag a wire out of the Yes/No data plug on the Light sensor block and connect it to the A input data plug on the COMPARE block, as shown in Figure 17-5.

Drag another wire out of the Yes/No data plug on the Sound sensor block, and connect it to the B input data plug on the COMPARE block, as shown in Figure 17-6.

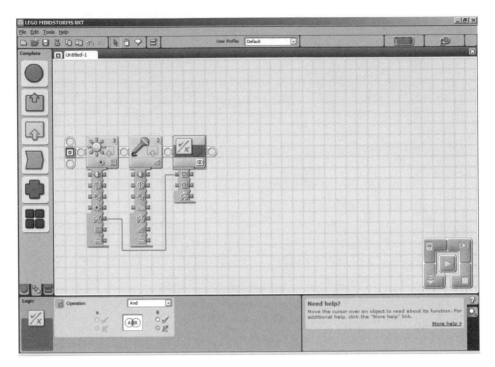

Figure 17-5. *Connect the Light sensor block to the COMPARE block.*

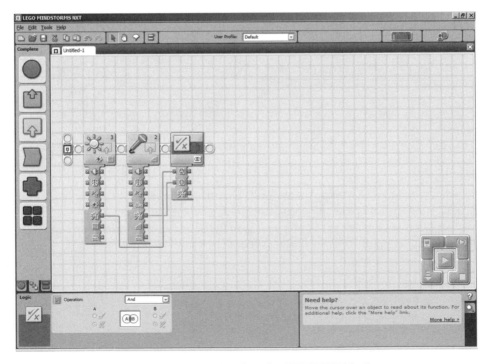

Figure 17-6. *Connect the Sound sensor block to the COMPARE block.*

Now, let me explain what is happening so far. The COMPARE block is taking a Yes/No response from the Light sensor. It is also taking a Yes/No response from the Sound sensor. By selecting the And option on the COMPARE block, we are forcing the COMPARE block to take the result in plug A (Yes or No) and the result in plug B (Yes or No) and add them together to create a single Yes/No response. I can already hear you asking, "How do you *add* Yes/No responses?"

Well, the answer is fairly simple and relies on the option you selected in that drop-down menu (the And, Or, Xor, and Not options):

And option: If you select the And option, *both* responses must be Yes for a final Yes result to be generated. If plug A is Yes and plug B is No, then the final result will be No. Likewise, if plug A is No and plug B is Yes, the final result will still be No. And if plug A is No and Plug B is No, the final result is No.

Or option: If you select the Or option, only *one* response must be Yes for a final Yes result to be generated. If plug A is Yes and plug B is No, then the final result will be Yes. Likewise, if plug A is No and plug B is Yes, the final result will still be Yes. If both plug A and plug B are both Yes, then the final result will be Yes. Only if plug A is No and Plug B is No, the final result is No.

Xor option: This is a weird one. If you select the Xor option, *only* one plug value *can be* Yes for a final Yes result to be generated. If plug A is Yes and plug B is No, then the final result will be Yes. Likewise, if plug A is No and plug B is Yes, the final result will still be Yes. However, if plug A and plug B are both Yes, the final result will be No. And if plug A and plug B are both No, the final result is No.

Not option: This is another strange one. This option doesn't really return a final value— it simply changes the Logic value input for plug A to its opposite. For example, if plug A is Yes, then the output for plug A will be No. This option reverses the Logic value for you and nothing else. Be aware that plug B will not work for the Not option.

Now, let's finish up our sample program. If you look back at Figure 17-6, we now have the LOGIC block ready to provide a Yes/No response (using a data wire).

If you recall, we are testing to see if the Sound sensor detects a value below 30 and the Light sensor detects a value below 20. If these conditions are both true, then SPOT will move forward three rotations. If either of these two conditions is not true, SPOT will not move.

So, our next step is to drop in a SWITCH block to test the condition of the LOGIC block. First, select Value from the Control section drop-down menu. Next, choose Logic from the Type section drop-down menu. We can leave the Flat View box checked, because we only have two possible options (True or False). This configuration is shown in Figure 17-7.

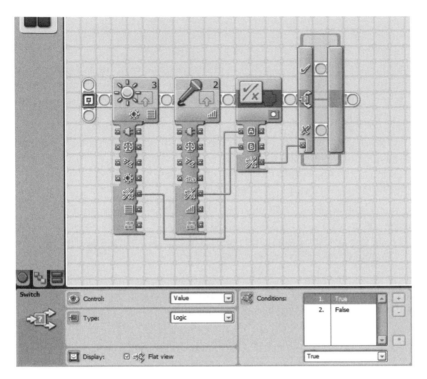

Figure 17-7. *A SWITCH block will use the LOGIC block output to control SPOT's actions.*

Now, here's where it can get a little tricky. If the Light sensor detects a light value below 30, then it sends a True value to the LOGIC block. If the Sound sensor detects a sound value below 20, then it sends a True value to the LOGIC block. We have configured the LOGIC block using the And option, because we want to test if both conditions are True. If they are, the LOGIC block will send a True value to the SWITCH block. If either of the conditions is False, the LOGIC block will send a False value to the SWITCH block.

So, all that's left is to drop in a MOVE block for the True condition in the SWITCH block, as shown in Figure 17-8.

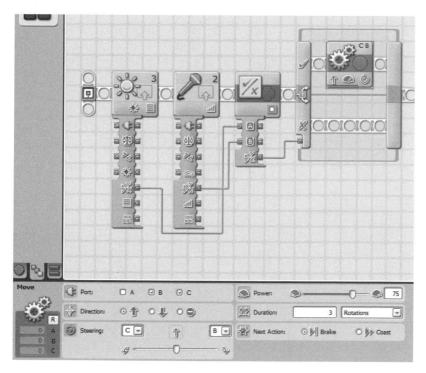

Figure 17-8. *A MOVE block is configured for three forward rotations.*

If the SWITCH block detects a True response from the LOGIC block, the MOVE block executes (three forward rotations), and the program ends. If the SWITCH block detects a False response from the LOGIC block, there are no additional blocks to run, and the program ends without SPOT moving.

And that's it! The LOGIC block is a useful tool for you to take two Logic data type responses (Yes/No or True/False) and "add" them together to produce one Logic data type. Are you wondering what you would do if, for example, you had four Logic data type inputs and needed to combine them? You would need to use two LOGIC blocks: each block would take two of the Logic data type input values and provide a final Logic response. These two Logic responses would then be combined using a third LOGIC block to obtain the true "final" Logic response. Confusing? A little. But when you start using the LOGIC block, you'll begin to see how it can be used with LOOP and SWITCH blocks to give your robots even better decision-making abilities.

■ ■ ■

CHAPTER 18

Title = Anything You Like

That's a strange title, isn't it? You can pick anything you like and make it the title. But that doesn't mean the material covered in this chapter will change. Nope, this chapter covers a special type of block called the VARIABLE block. You'll find this block useful when you need to store a piece of information for later use. So let's take a look.

The VARIABLE Block

Let's imagine for just a moment that you want to give SPOT some information to remember. This information consists of some words, a few numbers, and a couple of logical True/False values. SPOT has the ability to place each piece of information in a virtual folder that exists in his memory. Here's the pseudo-code:

Me: SPOT, will you please store the words "pizza" and "cheesecake" in your memory?

Me: SPOT, I also need you to store the numbers "50" and "200" in your memory.

Me: SPOT, will you also please store one logical "True" and one logical "False" in your memory?

Now, before we convert this pseudo-code to an NXT-G program, I need to tell you a little bit about how an NXT-G program stores information, changes it, and retrieves it. All of this is done using the VARIABLE block.

A VARIABLE block can do one of two things:

- Information can be *written to* a virtual folder that is stored in memory.

- Information can be *read from* a virtual folder that is stored in memory.

These virtual folders are also known as *variables*. An NXT-G variable can only be configured to hold one of three types of data: Text, Number, or Logic (True or False).

Text is easy enough; my pseudo-code tells SPOT to store "pizza" and "cheesecake," but it could just as easily have told SPOT to store the letter "A" or the sentence "My name is SPOT."

Numbers are even easier: when an NXT-G VARIABLE block is configured to hold a number, it can *only* be a positive or negative integer. Numbers such as 4.5 or –10.2 will be rounded to the nearest integer (5 and –10 for my examples).

Logic values only have two choices: True or False. An NXT-G VARIABLE block configured to hold a logical value can hold *only* True or False and nothing else.

OK, now it's time to take a look at the VARIABLE block. This block is found on the Complete Palette on the Data fly-out menu. Select the VARIABLE block, and drop it on the beam (see Figure 18-1).

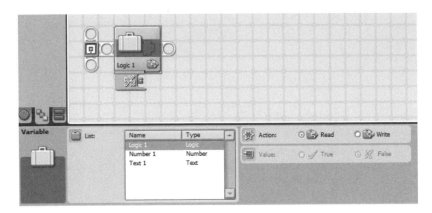

Figure 18-1. *The VARIABLE block and its configuration panel*

I mentioned to you that information can be *read from* or *written to* a VARIABLE block. In Figure 18-1, you'll notice that, by default, the first time you drop a block on the beam it is configured to Read (in the Action section) a Logic Type value. The variable also has a Name assigned to it: Logic 1.

This means that if True or False is stored in the variable, this value can be *read from* the variable. Notice that the Value section is grayed out; it isn't available for you to edit. Also notice that the default value selected in the Value section is False.

Before I show you how to change this, select the variable named Number 1 in the VARIABLE block's configuration panel (see Figure 18-2).

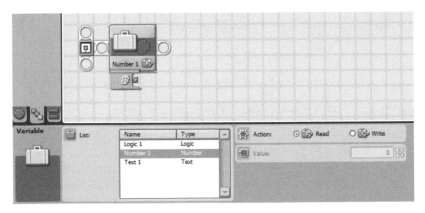

Figure 18-2. *The VARIABLE block with Number 1 selected as the variable name*

If you choose Number 1 as the variable name, you'll see that the default value stored is zero (0). This number is the value that will be *read from* the variable named Number 1.

Next, choose Text 1 in the VARIABLE block's configuration panel (see Figure 18-3).

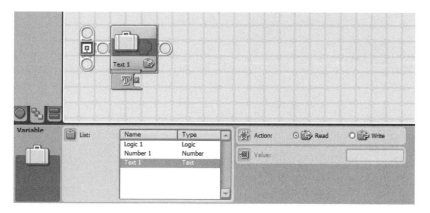

Figure 18-3. *The VARIABLE block with Text 1 selected as the variable name*

If you choose Text 1 as the variable name, the default value stored is blank; there is no text stored in the Text 1 variable.

In Figures 18-1, 18-2, and 18-3, notice also that the each of the blocks has only one output data plug. This matches what we know about a VARIABLE block with the Action section configured to Read. The variables can *only* be *read from*; other blocks (a DISPLAY block, for example) would use a data wire from this output data plug as input. This is "reading from" the variable.

I want to make sure you understand this concept, so take a look at Figure 18-4, and I'll explain it further.

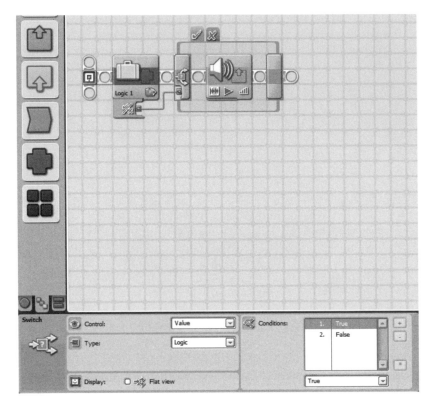

Figure 18-4. *A VARIABLE block providing its variable value to another block*

In Figure 18-4, I've connected a VARIABLE block called Logic 1 to a SWITCH block. The SWITCH block's configuration panel is visible in Figure 18-4, and you can see that I've configured it to check for a Logic value in the Type section. When the program is executed, the SWITCH block will *read* the value from the VARIABLE block. If the value is True, the SWITCH block will execute the SOUND block I've dropped in the True tab. If the value is False, the SWITCH block will execute a MOVE block that I dropped in the False tab.

Now, that example involved reading the data directly from the VARIABLE block. What if I want to put some data in? Then I'd have to *write* some data into the block. Here is how you do it.

Take a look at Figure 18-5. In this figure, I've selected Write in the Action section.

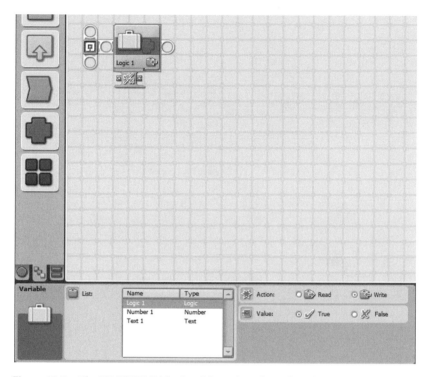

Figure 18-5. *The VARIABLE block with Write selected in the Action section*

In Figure 18-5, I can change the logic value. Remember that the default is False, so I've changed it to True. Did you also notice the input data plug that was added on the data hub? This means that I could actually have the True or False value determined by a data wire from another block. (In this example, the data wire *must* carry a logic value of True or False; anything else would give me a broken wire that wouldn't work. Likewise, if the List section has Number or Text selected, the input data wire *must* be providing a data type of the selected item.)

Figure 18-6 shows the configuration panels for the Number 1 and Text 1 blocks. I'm including them, because I want you to see how you can modify the data when the Action option is set to Write. For the Number 1 variable, you can type either a positive or a negative integer in the Value field. For the Text 1 variable, you can type words, sentences, or even entire paragraphs in the Value field.

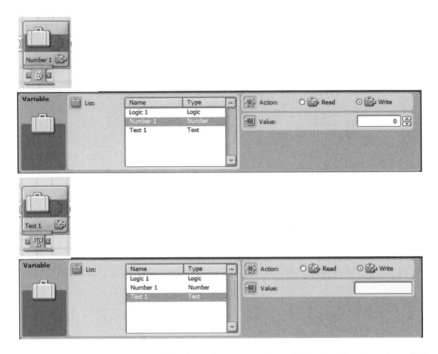

Figure 18-6. *The VARIABLE block with Write selected for the Number 1 and Text 1 variables*

After you've modified the data in a variable block, you can either close the variable by selecting Read in the Action menu (this prevents the data from being changed) or leave the block alone. If you choose to leave the Action section option as Write, you can drag a data wire from another block to the input data plug on the variable block (just remember that the type of data wire going into the input data plug must match the type of data the variable is configured to hold—Text, Number, or Logic).

Now, let's go back to the original pseudo-code I gave SPOT:

Me: SPOT, will you please store the words "pizza" and "cheesecake" in your memory?

Me: SPOT, I also need you to store the numbers "50" and "200" in your memory.

Me: SPOT, will you also please store one logical "True" and one logical "False" in your memory?

Do you see a problem? I've got two pieces of text to store and two number values. I already know that a variable block can only hold *one* piece of data. If I store the number 50, for example, in the Number 1 variable, where will I store the number 200? And I can store "pizza" in the Text 1 variable, but what about "cheesecake?"

The answer is simple. NXT-G allows you to create as many variables as you need. You can even rename a variable from something like Text 1 to something easier to remember like "Food", or Number 1 to something like "Test Scores". Here's how it's done.

If you need to create another variable, start by clicking the Edit menu at the top of the NXT-G software. Click the menu option labeled Define Variables.

A small window, like the one shown in Figure 18-7, opens.

Figure 18-7. *The Edit Variables window allows you to create new variables.*

Click the Create button, and a new variable will appear in the List section with a default name like MyVariable_1 (see Figure 18-8).

Figure 18-8. *Your new variable appears in the List section.*

You can change the name of the variable by typing a new name in the Name field. Select the type of data the variable will contain in the drop-down menu in the Datatype section. I've named my new variable Test Scores and configured it to hold a Number (see Figure 18-9). You can click the Create button again to make another variable. Click the Close button when you are finished.

Figure 18-9. *Give the new variable a Name and a Datatype to hold.*

Now, when you drop a VARIABLE block on the beam, you'll notice that your new variable appears as a selection in the List section (see Figure 18-10). Using this method, you can create as many Text, Number, and Logic variables as you need.

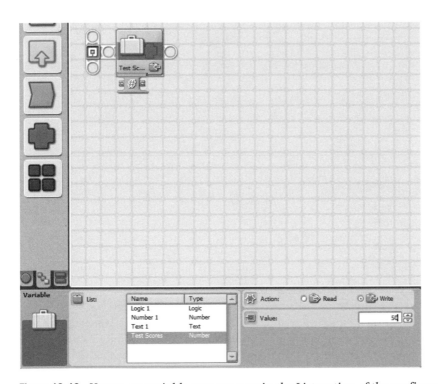

Figure 18-10. *Your new variable now appears in the List section of the configuration panel.*

OK, now you know how to put data into a variable (Write) and how to get data from a variable (Read). You also know how to create additional variables. The last thing I want to cover in this chapter is how to use variables throughout your programs.

Here's a bit of pseudo-code for SPOT:

Me: SPOT, I want you to wait for me to press and release the Enter button (orange button) for 3 seconds.

Me: If I press and release the button, display "Pressed" on the screen.

Me: If I do not press and release the button, display "Not Pressed" on the screen.

I'll first start off with a WAIT block configured to loop for 3 seconds (see Figure 18-11).

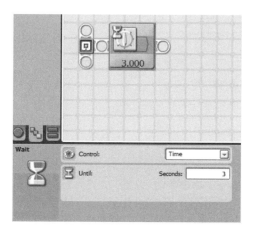

Figure 18-11. *The WAIT block is configured to loop for 3 seconds.*

I'll next drop in an NXT BUTTONS SENSOR block and configure it to detect the press and release (Bumped) of the Enter button (see Figure 18-12).

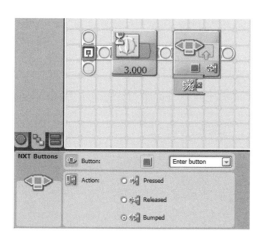

Figure 18-12. *The NXT BUTTONS SENSOR block will monitor the Enter button.*

I created a new VARIABLE block called "Pressed" that holds a Logic value. I next drop a VARIABLE block after the NXT BUTTONS SENSOR block. I choose my new variable, Pressed, and in the Action section, I choose Write. I also drag a data wire out of the NXT BUTTONS SENSOR block's output data plug into the input data plug on the VARIABLE block (see Figure 18-13).

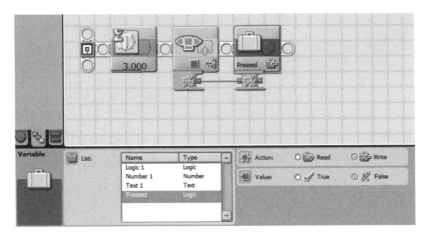

Figure 18-13. *The variable Pressed will hold True or False.*

If the Enter button is pressed and released during the first 3 seconds, the NXT BUTTONS SENSOR block will detect the press and release and change the logic value to True. A value of True or False will continue to be written to the Pressed variable block until the 3 seconds expire. When the program starts, the initial value will be False, but it can change anytime to True if the Enter button is bumped.

When the WAIT block ends (after 3 seconds), we need to display "Pressed" or "Not Pressed" on the LCD screen. To do this, we'll drop in another VARIABLE block. This time I'm going to choose my Pressed variable again, but I'm changing its Action section option to Read (see Figure 18-14).

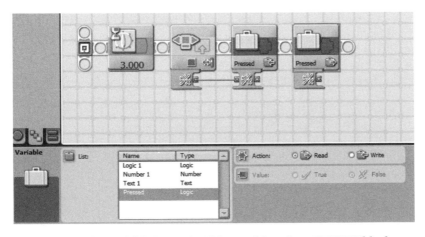

Figure 18-14. *The variable Pressed will be read from by a SWITCH block.*

Now, I drop in a SWITCH block and configure it to read a Logic value (see Figure 18-15), and I've turned off Flat view so the SWITCH block is visible in its tabbed format. I've also dragged a data wire from the VARIABLE block to the SWITCH block that contains the value True or False.

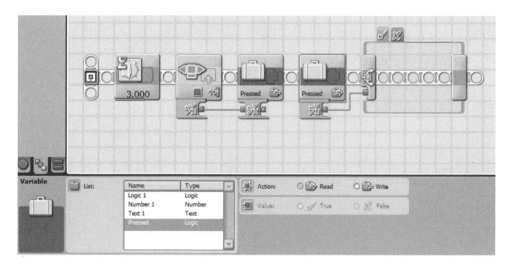

Figure 18-15. *The SWITCH block will read the Pressed variable's value.*

In the True tab, I place a DISPLAY block that clears the LCD screen and puts the word "Pressed" on the screen (see Figure 18-16).

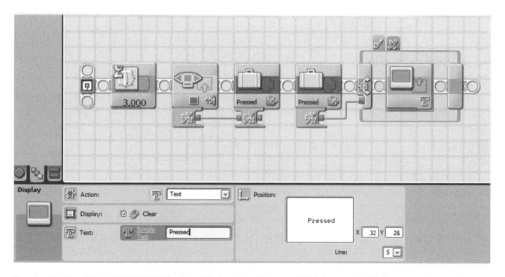

Figure 18-16. *This DISPLAY block will display "Pressed" if the variable has a value of True.*

On the False tab, I place another DISPLAY block that clears the LCD screen and puts the words "Not Pressed" on the screen (see Figure 18-17).

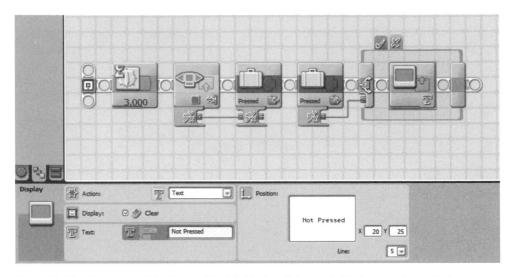

Figure 18-17. *The words "Not Pressed" will display if the variable has a value of False.*

Finally, I drop in an NXT BUTTON WAIT block to wait until the left button is pressed; this will give me time to view the results on the screen (see Figure 18-18).

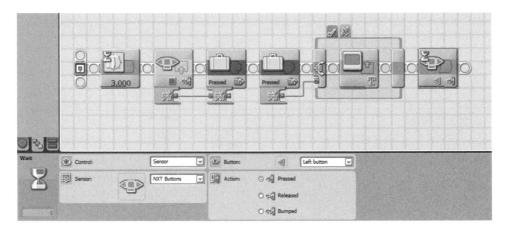

Figure 18-18. *If I press the left button, the program will end.*

Now run the program. Try it a few times—press and release the Enter button, or don't press and release it. Your decision to bump or not bump the button will be converted to a True or False value that is written to the Pressed variable. After 3 seconds, the Pressed variable is read by the SWITCH block, and the proper text is written on the LCD screen.

Variables are a powerful way for your robot to store away information—and to use that data later. Once the variable has been created and data written to it, that data will be available anytime you need it—well, at least until the program ends. If you want to store data for use after the program ends and/or after the power has been turned off, you'll need a different type of block; we'll discuss that later in Chapter 22. But in the next chapter, I'll show you how to use the TEXT block.

CHAPTER 19

■ ■ ■

Basic Text

For a chapter dealing with words, this one won't be too wordy. See? It even has a short introduction. You're going to learn to use the TEXT block to give your robot the ability to combine text into sentences and letters into words.

The TEXT Block

Mindstorms NXT robots can make a lot of noise using the SOUND block. But if you want to give your robots control over the written word, you'll need to understand the TEXT block and how to use it properly (see Figure 19-1).

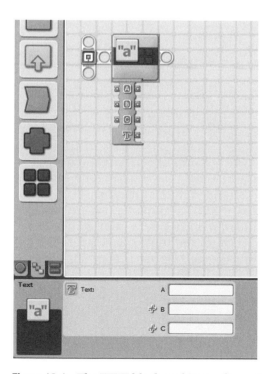

Figure 19-1. *The TEXT block and its configuration panel*

Here's another programming word for you to add to your list: *string* (and I don't mean the kind you use to fly a kite).

"String" is a term that's been around in programming circles forever and is fairly simple to define. A string is a collection of letters, numbers, spaces, special characters, or a combination of any of them. Here are five examples:

- THISISASTRINGOFTEXT

- So is this.

- 123456789

- !@#$%^&*( )

- These are all strings, including this one.

The reason I've introduced you to the concept of a string is that the TEXT block has the ability to take up to three different strings and merge them into one larger string value.

Look again at Figure 19-1. The TEXT block can hold three string values: A, B, and C. Notice that all three strings can be entered manually (by you, the programmer) or they can be submitted to the TEXT block using the input data plugs. Also, keep in mind that the value A will always be on the far left, B in the middle, and C on the right. You cannot change the order in which the three strings will be combined.

As an example, take a look at Figure 19-2.

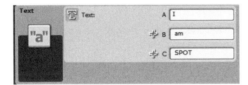

Figure 19-2. *Three string values for the TEXT block*

For value A, the text I entered is "I", with no spaces. Value B contains " am" (with a leading space), and value C is " SPOT" (with a leading space). The leading spaces will keep the combined text from looking like "IamSPOT"; instead, the combined text will look like "I am SPOT" when displayed on the screen. Once the text items are combined, how do I display the new string on the screen? I'll first add in a DISPLAY block to show the text on the screen (see Figure 19-3). I drag a wire from the output Text data plug (of the TEXT block) into the input Text data plug (on the DISPLAY block). The output Text data plug provides the combined text from A, B, and C.

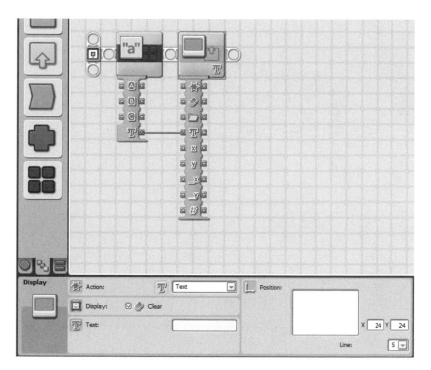

Figure 19-3. *Three string values combined and sent to the DISPLAY block*

Next, I add a TIME WAIT block, so I can view the text before the program ends and the text disappears; I'll configure the WAIT block for 10 seconds (see Figure 19-4).

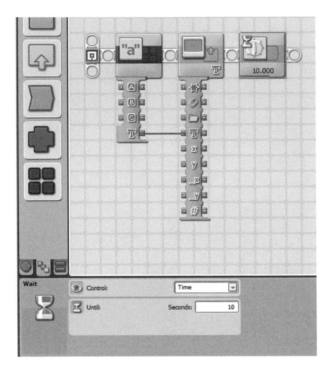

Figure 19-4. *This WAIT block gives me time to view the results on the screen.*

When I run the program, it now displays "I am SPOT" on the LCD screen. Earlier in the book (in Chapter 18), I showed you how to use the VARIABLE block. You could use this block to send text to the TEXT block using the input data plugs (A, B, and/or C). To do this, you would configure three VARIABLE blocks to each hold a bit of text. Drag a wire out of each VARIABLE block into ports A, B, and C and let the TEXT block do the rest!

Continue on to the next chapter, where I'll show you how to program your robot with some basic math skills.

CHAPTER 20

■ ■ ■

Basic Math

Don't you just love short chapters? Well, I promise this is going to be another extremely short chapter. So get ready to add another programming block to your collection of tools— we're going to turn our bot into a calculator.

The MATH Block

Your bots can do some very simple math: addition, subtraction, multiplication, and division. Take a look at Figure 20-1, which shows the MATH block and its configuration panel.

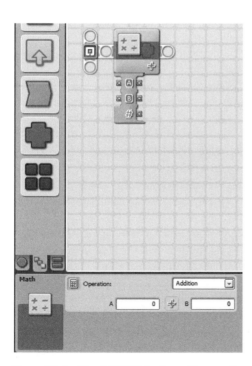

Figure 20-1. *The MATH block and its configuration panel*

The MATH block uses two values: A and B. These values can be positive or negative integers. An *integer* is a whole number with no decimal values. If you attempt to enter in a number such as –4.3 or 10.8 the MATH block will round the values up or down to the nearest integer (–4 and 11 for my examples).

In the Operation section, there is a drop-down menu for you to select the type of operation to be performed. If you go ahead and click the drop-down menu, you should see the following options:

- *Addition*: This option will add values A and B.

- *Subtraction*: This option will subtract value B from value A.

- *Multiplication*: This option will multiply value A by value B.

- *Division*: This option will divide value A by value B.

Notice in Figure 20-1 that I've opened the data hub on the MATH block. There are two input data wire plugs (one for value A and one for value B) and three output data wire plugs. The MATH block requires two integer values: if A or B is left blank, its value defaults to 0. These numbers can be entered manually by typing a value for A and a value for B in the configuration panel, or they can be provided to the MATH block by running one data wire into plug A and another data wire into plug B (see Figure 20-2).

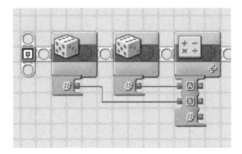

Figure 20-2. *The MATH block can receive data wires for values of A and B.*

In Figure 20-2, I've created a sample program that creates two random numbers (generated by two RANDOM blocks). Each RANDOM block uses its output data plug to run a wire into the A and B input data plugs on the MATH block.

You should understand that you really can't do anything with the MATH block without having its data hub open. The reason for this is simple: no matter what operation (addition, subtraction, multiplication, or division) you choose to perform on values A and B, the answer can only be obtained from the Result data plug (using a data wire).

Once values A and B have been added together, I want to see the answer on the LCD screen. To do this, I have to first convert the number to text. I drop in a NUMBER TO TEXT block (see Figure 20-3) and drag a data wire from the Result data plug on the MATH block into the Number data plug on the NUMBER TO TEXT block.

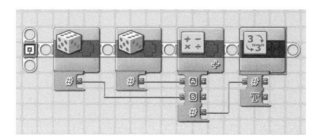

Figure 20-3. *The NUMBER TO TEXT block will convert the numeric answer to text.*

In order for me to see the answer on the Brick's LCD screen, I drag a data wire out of the Text data plug on the NUMBER TO TEXT block and into the Text data plug on the DISPLAY block; see Figure 20-4 (remember to change the DISPLAY block to show Text). I'm also adding in a small WAIT block, so I can see the results before they disappear off the screen.

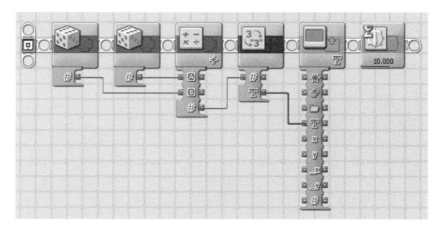

Figure 20-4. *The DISPLAY block will show the result on the LCD screen.*

And that's it for the MATH block! Remember, value A and value B must be positive or negative integers and will default to *zero* (0) if you don't configure a value for them. And if you plan on displaying the results of your MATH block, you'll need to convert the number to text before sending it to a DISPLAY block. Have fun! Up next, I'll show you how to prevent your robots from falling asleep.

CHAPTER 21

■■■

Staying Alive

Another short chapter? Of course! You can learn something and then get back to playing around with your NXT robots. But you won't get to play much if your robots keep falling asleep. This chapter will show you how to keep your robots working, even if the Sleep option on the Brick has been set to a short period of time like 2 minutes or 5 minutes.

The KEEP ALIVE Block

Your NXT Brick has a built-in feature that automatically turns off your robot after a certain amount of time has passed with no activity. This Sleep timer is configured on the Brick, and you can choose for the Brick to shut down after 2, 5, 10, 30, or 60 minutes of inactivity, or you can choose Never.

The Sleep timer is a useful feature, and you should definitely set it to a reasonable time. It can help save battery power if you accidentally leave the Brick turned on. If a program finishes executing, for example, and the robot stops moving while you're away for a little bit, the Sleep timer can make sure your robot turns itself off.

The KEEP ALIVE block and its configuration panel are shown in Figure 21-1.

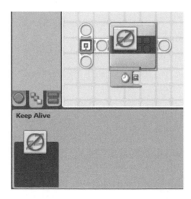

Figure 21-1. *The KEEP ALIVE block and its configuration panel*

Notice that the configuration panel is blank! There are no settings to configure with the KEEP ALIVE block.

Here's how it works: During the execution of your program, if at any time a KEEP ALIVE block is executed, the Sleep timer resets to its initial starting time. So, if you configured your Brick for a 5-minute Sleep timer and 1 minute into the program a KEEP ALIVE block is encountered, the Sleep timer will reset to 5 minutes.

Now, to make this useful, you'll probably need to place the KEEP ALIVE block in a location where it will frequently be executed. The best location is a LOOP block that will occasionally (or continually) run the blocks inside it, including the KEEP ALIVE block. This is one method for continually resetting the Sleep timer.

An example is shown in Figure 21-2.

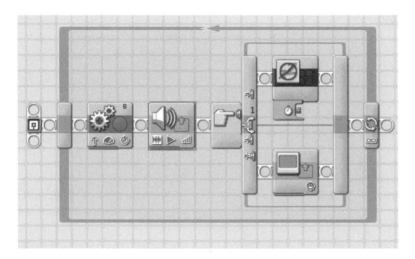

Figure 21-2. *Put a KEEP ALIVE inside a LOOP, and you can repeatedly reset the Sleep timer.*

In this simple program, the bot will spin around a few times, say "Hello", and then do it again and again and again . . . if the Touch sensor button is ever pressed, the SWITCH block will execute the KEEP ALIVE block, which resets the Sleep timer. If the button is never pressed, the bot will eventually turn off when the default Sleep timer value has been reached.

This is important: always check the Sleep timer setting on your Brick before running a program. Once the time has expired, the program will stop. This happens frequently when the Sleep timer is set to 2 minutes or 5 minutes, so double-check this before running a program, and be certain to set the Sleep timer to a setting that is longer than you expect the program to run.

To close out this chapter, the last item I want to mention about the KEEP ALIVE block is that it does have an output data plug in its data hub. This data plug will *only* supply a Number data type, and that number will always be the Sleep timer default value in milliseconds (1,000 milliseconds = 1 second). You might not find this data plug very useful, but it could be used as input to a COMPARE block that looks to see which is greater—a value from one of the Brick's three internal timers or the default Sleep timer value. Depending on the condition of the COMPARE block, your bot might perform some final action before letting the robot shut down using a STOP block *or*, as mentioned earlier, it might execute a KEEP ALIVE block to reset the Sleep timer value.

Well, that's it for the KEEP ALIVE block. Up next in Chapter 22 is the FILE ACCESS block. You'll learn how to program your bot to store data in files that can be accessed at any time, now or later.

CHAPTER 22

■■■

Your Own Filing Cabinet

In Chapter 18, I showed you how to use VARIABLE blocks to hold data such as Numbers and Text. But the problem with the VARIABLE block is that when the program ends, the data disappears! Even worse, if the batteries die or the power is turned off on your robot while it's running, the VARIABLE blocks all lose whatever values they were holding.

Fortunately, your NXT robots have access to a block that can hold data in memory longer—even if you turn off the robot's power or the program ends. This data is stored in a file that is kept in the NXT Brick's memory, and it stays there until you delete it, just like a program.

The FILE ACCESS Block

The FILE ACCESS block is shown in Figure 22-1 along with its configuration panel.

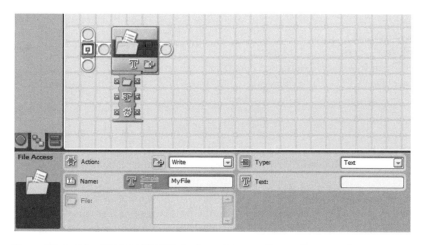

Figure 22-1. *The FILE ACCESS block and its configuration panel*

Now, before I get into showing you how to use this block, let me first explain some simple rules that you must obey when using the FILE ACCESS block:

Rule 1: The block can only hold Number or Text data, not Logic.

Rule 2: The block can perform four actions: Read, Write, Close, and Delete.

Rule 3: Each FILE ACCESS block can only perform one of the actions; this means that you need to use one FILE ACCESS block per action type.

Rule 4: When you write data to a file, the data is added to the end of any existing data already in the file.

Suppose that your Text data file has the following data stored in it: 15429823. Now, what will happen if you add 34 to it? Well, according to rule 4, the file will now be holding 1542982334. The 34 is *appended* to the end.

There are just a few more rules for you to remember:

Rule 5: To read the data written to a file, you must first close the file.

Rule 6: To overwrite the file (but keep the same filename), you must delete the file and create a new one with the same name.

The FILE ACCESS block does require some experimentation to learn how to properly use it. I highly encourage you to perform the following examples and then experiment by making changes. Try to read a mixture of values (of Number and Text types). Next, close the file and try opening it again and reading back your values. By playing with the block, you'll quickly figure out how best to use it with your own robots.

But for now, let me go over the basics of how to use the block.

Let's start with the Action section in the configuration panel. The Action section has a drop-down menu with four options: Read, Write, Close, and Delete. Easy enough—choose the Read option to read the contents of a file; choose the Write option to write data to a file; choose the Close option to close the file; and choose Delete to delete the file.

The Name section is where you specify the name of the file you will be working with (you might be writing, reading, closing, or deleting it). If you are creating a new file, keep the name short and unique but descriptive enough so you'll remember what kind of data it holds. Good examples are "RightTurns" (it could hold the total number of right turns a robot makes) and "TeamName" (this could hold a team's name for use in different programs).

The File section will list any files that currently exist on the NXT Brick when the Brick is connected and communicating with the software. You can choose a file from this list rather than specifying a new filename.

The Type section has a drop-down with two options: Number and Text. Choosing Number creates a Number section where you can type in a numeric value or use the small buttons to increase or decrease the number (if you are writing to the file). Choosing Text will create a Text section where you can type in a bit of text (also if you are writing to a file).

If you are reading from a file, you must specify if you are reading a Number or Text value from the file. If the file contains 1234, for example, and you select to read a text value, the data will be treated as text and not as a number. Keep that in mind, and remember to always select the proper type of data to read or write to a file.

If you are closing a file, this simply protects the file from being written or deleted. It's a good practice to always close a file when you are finished using it and before opening a different file.

Let me give you a small example of a program that uses the FILE ACCESS block.

First, I'll create a new file called LuckyNumber, as shown in Figure 22-2. I'll choose to write 15 as a Number value into the file.

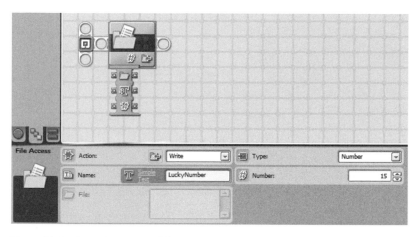

Figure 22-2. *Creating a new file*

I'll need to close the file after the number has been written to the file. This will allow me to later read the data. So I'll add another FILE ACCESS block that closes the file (see Figure 22-3).

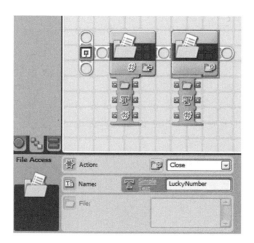

Figure 22-3. *Closing the file will allow me to read from it later.*

Now, here's some pseudo-code for SPOT:

Me: SPOT, I've stored a file in your memory called LuckyNumber. I want you to move forward three rotations and then display my lucky number on your LCD screen.

Here's how the program will look. First, I'll drop in a MOVE block that will move SPOT forward three rotations (see Figure 22-4).

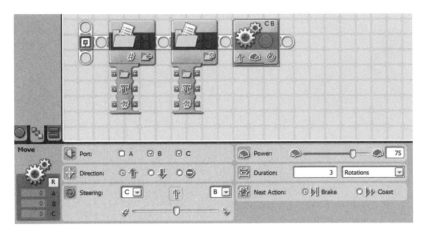

Figure 22-4. *Move forward three rotations.*

Now, I'll need to read the number stored in the LuckyNumber file and have SPOT display that value on his LCD screen. Fortunately, I can use a NUMBER TO TEXT block that will take a Number value and send that to a DISPLAY block. So, my first step is to read that value from the file. This is done by dropping in another FILE ACCESS block and reading the data (see Figure 22-5).

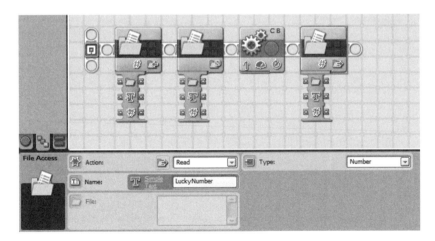

Figure 22-5. *Read the value stored in the file.*

Now, I need to drop in a NUMBER TO TEXT block and configure it to read the value stored in the file. I'll then pass this Text value on to a DISPLAY block. This is shown in Figure 22-6 along with the final WAIT block and its configuration panel.

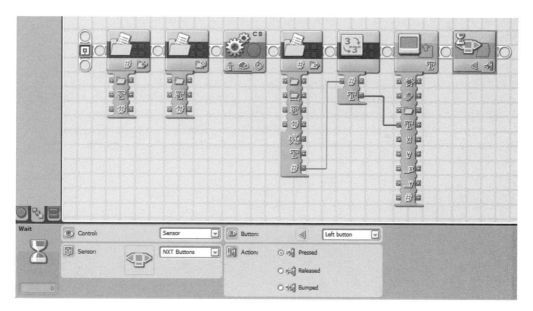

Figure 22-6. *Read the value stored in the file.*

Be sure to notice that there are two data plugs that have the pound (number) symbol: #. One is used to provide input to the FILE ACCESS block, and another is used as an output data plug. Figure 22-6 shows a data wire running from the output data plug. Be careful to select the correct one when using a FILE ACCESS block, or you'll receive a broken wire. Once this is completed, the FILE ACCESS block will provide the number stored as data that can be read by the NUMBER TO TEXT block. You'll just have to test this to prove it to yourself. The NUMBER TO TEXT block provides this to the DISPLAY block; the program waits for you to press the Left button (using the final WAIT block), and the program then ends.

The FILE ACCESS block is a great way for you to store data that your robot obtains during its explorations. You could use files to store things like number of motor rotations and left and right turns it makes. Your robot could later read from these files and find its way back home. There are many ways to use files stored on your Brick, and now you know how to create them, add to them, and delete them.

Before I close out this chapter, I want to mention a couple of useful tips. The first is to always get in a habit of closing your file. By doing this, you reset the file, and any values stored inside will be read in order (first to last). If you are using a FILE ACCESS block in other programs, I also suggest that you place a FILE ACCESS block at the beginning of the program and configure it to close the file. Again, do this to ensure that the file's data will be read in proper order.

Because the data stored in a file is in sequential order, to read another value simply requires adding another FILE ACCESS block set to Read, *or* you can place a FILE ACCESS block inside a LOOP block so that every time the program loops, the FILE ACCESS block will read the next value in the file.

Finally, do remember that the file has an end. When the end of the file is reached, the FILE ACCESS block will not read any more values. To determine if this is happening, the FILE ACCESS block has a very useful Error data plug that returns a True or False Logic value. You can drag a data wire out of the Error data plug and use it as a condition to monitor. For example, a LOOP block could be configured to break when a True value is received from the Error data plug—the loop breaks and the program continues.

This chapter has only touched lightly on the power of the FILE ACCESS block. Believe me; there are many more uses for this block, and you'll find that giving your robots the ability to record data (and later retrieve it) will be a powerful tool. You can use it to keep track of light values, left and right turns, and more. Play around and experiment with the FILE ACCESS block to learn the little tricks that will allow you to give your robot a long-term memory!

Up next, make sure your Light and Sound sensors are working properly using the CALIBRATION block.

CHAPTER 23

Calibration

When it comes to the Sound and Light sensors, you will find that the minimum and maximum values that these two sensors can change from environment to environment. If your robot, for example, is located in a well-lit room, the minimum value (darkest spot in the room) will be substantially different from the minimum value the sensor obtains in a poorly lit room.

This chapter will show you how to use the CALIBRATE block, so you can trust the values your Sound and Light sensors are receiving.

The CALIBRATE Block

The CALIBRATE block is only available for the Light sensor (both NXT and RIS versions) and the Sound sensor. Figure 23-1 shows the basic CALIBRATE block and its configuration panel.

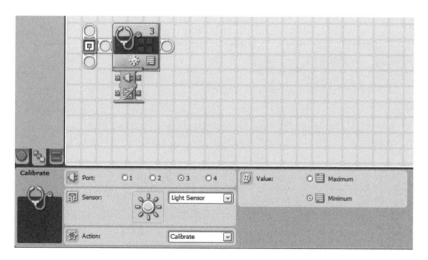

Figure 23-1. *The CALIBRATE block and its configuration panel*

Using the drop-down menu in the Sensor section, you can choose Light sensor or Sound sensor. The Port section is simple enough; just select the port number where the sensor you wish to calibrate is plugged in.

The Action section has a drop-down menu with two options: Calibrate and Delete. Calibrate is the typical option you will select, but if you wish to reset the Minimum or Maximum values for a sensor, choose the Delete option to delete the current settings, and then use additional CALIBRATE blocks to obtain new values.

The Value section is where you will choose to Calibrate or Delete the Minimum or Maximum value. This is important to remember: one CALIBRATE block is required to calibrate (or delete) the minimum value and an additional CALIBRATE block is needed to calibrate (or delete) the maximum value. However, if you choose to only one CALIBRATE block, the good news is that calibrating one value (the minimum value, for example) will automatically calibrate the other value. To be safe, though, it's probably best to always use one CALIBRATE block for the minimum value and another for the maximum value.

There is one additional feature of the CALIBRATE block you need to know about, and it relates to multiple Sound or Light sensors. If you are using two or more of the same type of sensor, the minimum and maximum values obtained from two CALIBRATE blocks will apply to *all* sensors of that type. There is no need, for example, to have six CALIBRATE blocks for three Sound sensors—one block can be used to set the minimum values for all three Sound sensors and another block to set the maximum values.

And how do you actually calibrate your robot's sensors to the environment where it will be performing actions? The answer is simple, and I'll give you examples for both the Sound sensor and the Light sensor.

Let's look at the Light sensor first. If you've built a robot with a Light sensor (or multiple Light sensors) and you want to calibrate them to the current surroundings, the first thing you need to do is place two CALIBRATE blocks inside your program, preferably at the beginning of the program. The help documentation included with your NXT kit has a great suggestion, and I'm going to use it here with a sample of the NXT-G program code.

Take a look at Figure 23-2.

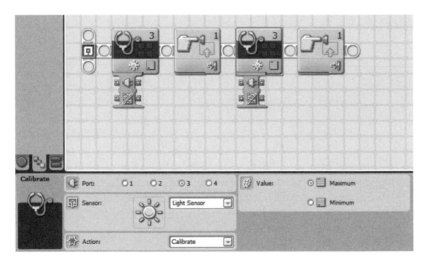

Figure 23-2. *Calibrating a Light sensor*

In this example, I've placed two CALIBRATE blocks. The first one is set to Calibrate the Minimum value for the Light sensor. The second block is set to Calibrate the Maximum value for the Light sensor. After the first CALIBRATE block, I've placed a TOUCH SENSOR WAIT block that simply waits for the sensor's button to be pressed. I've done the same thing for the second

CALIBRATE block. This bit of NXT-G code can be placed at the beginning of your NXT-G program for your robot.

Now, the first thing I do is place the robot in the darkest (or least lighted) area of the room. When I've done this, I press the Touch sensor button. This allows the first CALIBRATE block to obtain the minimum value for the room.

Next, I take the robot and place it in the brightest area of the room. I press the Touch sensor button, and the second CALIBRATE block obtains the Maximum value for the room.

And that's it! Now, if I've programmed my robot to use the Light sensor at any point in its program, the Light sensor should react properly based on any conditions I've programmed (such as "Turn Left if the Light sensor obtains a value over 30").

For the Sound sensor, I perform the exact same steps. Figure 23-3 shows the same NXT-G code but with the Sound sensor configured for calibration.

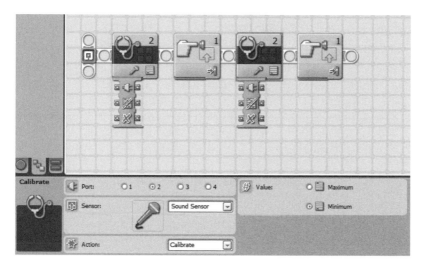

Figure 23-3. *Calibrating a Sound sensor*

In this example, I would try to place the robot in the quietest point in the room. This could be difficult, as I cannot predict factors such as observers or other potential sources of sound, but I'll do my best. I press the Touch sensor button, and the first CALIBRATE block will obtain the Minimum value for the Sound sensor. Next, I'll place the robot in what I think will be the noisiest part of the room and press the Touch sensor button. The Maximum value for the Sound sensor is now set.

One thing to note with the Sound sensor is the proximity of the sensor to the NXT motors. Keep in mind that when your robot is using any or all of its motors, the sound from the motors can influence the Sound sensor if you have programmed it to use the sound level for decision making. You'll have to experiment and test your robots to determine the proper settings to configure for your Sound sensor triggers. You might program SPOT to turn left if the sound level is less than 20, but the sound coming from the NXT motors might cause the Sound sensor to evaluate the sound level as 22 or 23 when all other conditions are correct for a left turn. That's why it always pays to *test, test, test.*

Well, that does it for the CALIBRATE block. In Chapter 24, I'm going to show you how to program your bot to reset its motors, which is useful if you are monitoring motor rotation, for example. Keep reading to find out how it works.

CHAPTER 24

■ ■ ■

Get Reset

This chapter covers the extremely simple RESET MOTOR block, which only does one thing, and that one thing is something you may rarely (or never) use. I have actually never found a strong use for it, but who knows? This may very well be the one block that you've been looking for to make your new robot function properly. So let's briefly cover the RESET MOTOR block, and I'll explain how it works.

The RESET MOTOR Block

The RESET MOTOR block is shown in Figure 24-1 along with its configuration panel.

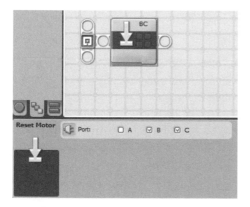

Figure 24-1. *The RESET MOTOR block and its configuration panel*

One of the first things you might notice about this block is that its configuration panel is extremely simple. You simply check the ports for the motors (A, B, and/or C) on which you wish to use the RESET MOTOR block. And why would you want to do this? I'll explain.

One of the great things about the NXT servo motors is the ability to pair them, so your robots can move in a more accurate straight line. The Brick sends the proper signal to motors B and C (I'm assuming you're using B and C for your movement control) and ensures that they spin at the same rate. By doing this, your robot is able to travel in fairly accurate straight lines. Imagine if one motor was spinning a little faster or farther than the other—your robot would end up moving in a not-so-straight line. Also, by pairing the motors, you can ensure that both motors are spinning with the same duration, such as 300 degrees or 2.5 rotations. This behavior is one of the advantages of the NXT motors.

Take a look at the following pseudo-code:

Me: SPOT, move forward 360 degrees and wait 3 seconds.

Me: Now, move forward 270 degrees and wait 3 seconds.

Me: Now, move forward 90 degrees and stop.

The NXT-G program for this pseudo-code looks like the one shown in Figure 24-2.

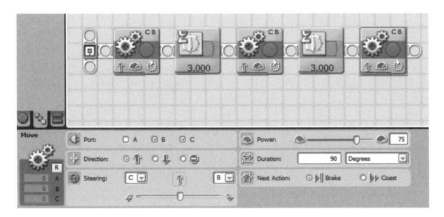

Figure 24-2. *An NXT-G program to move SPOT*

In the program, I've added three MOVE blocks and a couple of WAIT blocks. The first MOVE block moves SPOT forward 360 degrees, and then SPOT waits for 3 seconds. The second MOVE block moves him forward 270 degrees, and then he waits for 3 more seconds. Finally, the third MOVE block moves him forward 90 degrees, and he stops. In all, SPOT has moved forward 720 degrees, or 2 rotations, for motors B and C. Now, I also configured the first two MOVE blocks to Coast in the Next Action section and the third MOVE block to Brake. I did this because I want to demonstrate a little trick that your NXT Brick and its motors perform.

Let's say that after SPOT's first MOVE block executes, SPOT actually rolls forward 380 degrees with the slight coast. On SPOT's second movement, he rolls forward 278 degrees with the coast. Now, if SPOT's final movement forward is 97 degrees, he will have moved a total of 755 degrees, not the expected 720 degrees. But if you upload this program to SPOT and run it, you'll find that SPOT will actually move forward 720 degrees, or 2 rotations. How?

The Brick and motors keep track of the distance SPOT coasts and reduce the final movement of the third MOVE block (configured to Brake) to a value of 62 degrees, not 90 degrees. By reducing the final MOVE block to 62 degrees, SPOT is still able to move forward a total of 720 degrees with accuracy (if the final MOVE block was set to Coast instead of Brake, this accuracy could not be guaranteed). It is this "error correction" that the Brick and motors provide that allows your robot to make very precise movements.

But what if you don't care about the preciseness of the moves and want to shut off the "error correction" activity of the Brick and motors? Well, that's where the RESET MOTOR block comes into the picture.

Take a look at Figure 24-3, and you'll see SPOT's original program slightly modified.

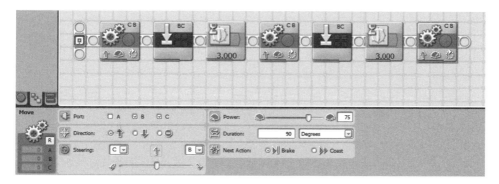

Figure 24-3. *Another NXT-G program to move SPOT*

In this program, SPOT will perform the same actions, but after the first MOVE block has been executed, the RESET MOTOR block will perform its action. Recall that your Brick and motors are communicating and keeping track of the number of degrees that you've programmed SPOT to move. If the first MOVE block causes SPOT to move forward 380 degrees, the RESET MOTOR block simply clears that value (resets to 0), and it's as if SPOT never moved at all. The second MOVE block may move SPOT forward another 277 degrees, but the second RESET MOTOR block resets that value to 0, too. Finally, the third MOVE block moves SPOT forward 90 degrees and then brakes. All in all, SPOT has moved forward a total of 747 degrees, not 720. SPOT moved an additional 27 degrees, because the "error correction" built into the motors has been disabled by the RESET MOTOR blocks.

And that's it for the RESET MOTOR block. If you decide that you're not concerned with your robot keeping track of its movement durations and prefer to use the Coast feature with your MOVE blocks (maybe to save battery power), then the RESET MOTOR block may be useful to you. But as I stated earlier, I've never actually found a good reason to use it.

Up next, we'll go over the SEND MESSAGE and RECEIVE MESSAGE blocks, and you'll learn how to program your NXT robot to communicate with other NXT robots.

CHAPTER 25

■ ■ ■

Messages

There may come a time when you'd like your NXT robot to be able to communicate and share information with other NXT robots. Or, if you have a second NXT kit, you could build a remote control for your robot and give it commands using the second NXT Brick.

To make all this happen requires a couple of blocks that will both be covered in this chapter. Many people find these blocks difficult or confusing, but they're really very simple if you understand the basic concept behind sending and receiving messages.

Of course, sending and receiving message requires that both NXT blocks be connected via a Bluetooth connection. Connecting two or more NXT Bricks via Bluetooth is not covered here, so if you need help with this task, check the built-in Help file with your NXT software; you can find instructions for connecting two or more NXT devices using Bluetooth by reading either the SEND MESSAGE or RECEIVE MESSAGE block's documentation.

The SEND MESSAGE Block

The SEND MESSAGE block is shown in Figure 25-1 along with its configuration panel.

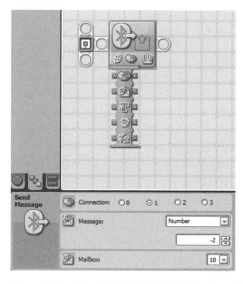

Figure 25-1. *The SEND MESSAGE block and its configuration panel*

There are a couple of items you really need to understand in the configuration panel. The first one is found in the Message section. The drop-down menu has three options: Text, Number, or Logic. By selecting one of these, you supply the correct type of message in the text box immediately below the drop-down menu. If you choose Text in the drop-down, the text box must contain some form of text content. Likewise, if you choose Number in the drop-down menu, the text box must contain a positive or negative integer value. And last, selecting Logic from the drop-down menu requires that you must select the True or False value.

Note As with most of the advanced NXT blocks, the SEND MESSAGE block can be configured to receive Text, Number, or Logic values using data wires, as shown in Figure 25-1. Note that the Connection data plug is a value between 0 and 3 and is used to identify the master or slave NXT device.

There really isn't much difference between the master and slave devices; both use Bluetooth to communicate, but I would suggest making the master the robot that will have the most responsibilities. An example is a robot that sends a signal to another robot to move or make a sound or take a sensor reading. Sometimes multiple robots will all be running the same program and sending signals back and forth; in this case, pick any robot as master and the remaining robots (up to three more) will be configured as slave devices. Since you have four possible values, it's possible to connect the slave Bricks to one master Brick. This is what will allow you to control up to three additional robots with a single NXT robot.

Now, this is a great way for one NXT Brick to send a single item to another Brick. One NXT Brick could, for example, monitor the number of times the Touch sensor is triggered and send this value to another robot. But what if you want to send even more information? What about sending the Light sensor's value as well as the number of rotations motor B has made to the second robot? Is this possible?

Well, if you think of each potential message as a variable (covered in Chapter 18), then the answer is, "Yes." The SEND MESSAGE and RECEIVE MESSAGE blocks allow for up to ten unique messages to be sent back and forth between Bricks using a concept called *mailboxes*.

Each NXT Brick has ten mailboxes, and each mailbox is numbered. The first mailbox is called Mailbox 1; the second mailbox is called Mailbox 2, and so on. If you look at the configuration panel for the SEND MESSAGE block, you'll see that the last section is called Mailbox, and it contains a drop-down menu. Select this drop-down menu, and you'll see that you can select from numbers 1 to 10. It's simple! When you place a Text, Number, or Logic value in Mailbox 3, for example, that value is held in that mailbox (remember, a Text value can be a single character or multiple characters but is still considered a single value to a mailbox). Up to five values can be held per mailbox, *but* the values held *must* be of the same type (Text, Number, or Logic). If, for example, a SEND MESSAGE block attempts to put a sixth value in Mailbox 5, the first value inserted into Mailbox 5 drops out and is lost. So be careful about putting too many values into a Mailbox before they are retrieved!

Now, can you guess how your second robot will retrieve a value held in a mailbox? If you said by using a RECEIVE MESSAGE block, you're right. Take a look at Figure 25-2, and you'll see the RECEIVE MESSAGE block and its configuration panel.

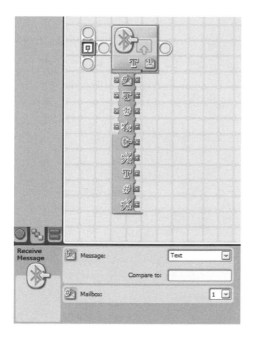

Figure 25-2. *The RECEIVE MESSAGE block and its configuration panel*

The RECEIVE MESSAGE block works similarly to the SEND MESSAGE block. Select the mailbox number from the drop-down menu in the Mailbox section. Again, the mailboxes are numbered 1 to 10. You must also select the type of data you are expecting to receive from the SEND MESSAGE block (Text, Number, or Logic) in the drop-down menu in the Message section.

You'll notice that in the Message section there is a "Compare to" text box. If you enter a value in this box, a True or False logic value will be determined, and using an output data wire, you can obtain this logic value to give it to another block. For example, if Mailbox 3 is holding a Number data type value of 250, your RECEIVE MESSAGE block is configured to read a Number value from Mailbox 3, and you've entered **250** in the "Compare to" text box, a True value will result from the comparison.

Now, for a quick example of a simple program, let's take the following pseudo-code and convert it to an NXT-G program:

Me: SPOT, move forward until your Ultrasonic sensor detects an object at least 10 inches in front of you.

Me: Read the value on your Light sensor.

Me: Send the Light sensor Intensity value to SPOT2 using Mailbox 3.

As you can see from Figure 25-3, I've created a simple program that causes SPOT to start moving forward (Unlimited duration) while monitoring his Ultrasonic sensor. When the Ultrasonic sensor is triggered, the second MOVE block stops motors B and C. The Light sensor takes a reading, and this value is sent to the SEND MESSAGE block using a data wire configured to hold a Number value.

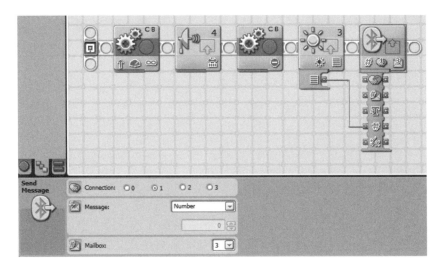

Figure 25-3. *A program using the SEND MESSAGE block*

Now, if I have a second robot (called SPOT2), I can convert the following pseudo-code into another NXT-G program that will obtain the Light sensor value:

Me: SPOT2, check Mailbox 3 for a Number value.

Me: Compare that value to your Light sensor reading.

Me: If your Light sensor reading matches the value in Mailbox 3, move forward eight rotations.

Now, take a look at Figure 25-4 to see how I've converted the pseudo-code to an NXT-G program.

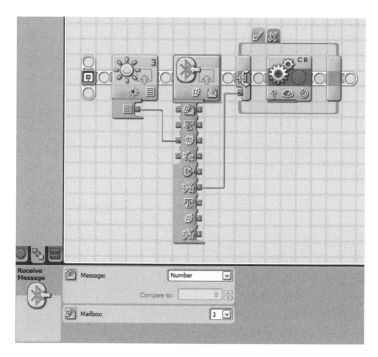

Figure 25-4. *A program using the RECEIVE MESSAGE block*

In this program, SPOT2's Light sensor takes a reading, and this value is passed to the RECEIVE MESSAGE block using a data wire. Now, when SPOT2 checks Mailbox 3 and reads the value, a comparison is made between the stored value and the value obtained by SPOT2's Light sensor. This comparison is done automatically, because a number value has been provided to the RECEIVE MESSAGE block's Number data port and a data wire has been dragged out of the RECEIVE MESSAGE block's Logic data port and into the SWITCH block. This setup forces the block to do a comparison of the two values (the one obtained by the Light sensor and the Number configured in the configuration panel). If these values are equal, a True value is passed to the SWITCH block. The True tab is shown in Figure 25-4 and includes a MOVE block that will move SPOT2 forward eight rotations if Mailbox 3's value and SPOT2's Light sensor values are identical.

The SEND MESSAGE block and the RECEIVE MESSAGE block are absolutely essential for two or more NXT robots to communicate and share information. This chapter has barely scratched the surface of what can be done using these two blocks. I mentioned earlier that with a second NXT kit, you can build a remote control for your robot. In order to build a useful remote control, you need to use the SEND MESSAGE blocks in your remote control to send numeric values to the robot. These values could represent the number of rotations or degrees for motors B and C to spin, for example. Or they could represent the speed/power of the motors to spin. There are numerous ways to do this, and there really is no incorrect method—just pick the one that works best for you.

Well, we've got one more item to cover; it's called the My Block. And you're going to find it very useful for creating small programs that can be used over and over again in future robots.

■■■

CHAPTER 26

My Block Is Your Block

Don't go crazy looking for an actual NXT-G block on the palettes called "My Block." It doesn't exist. My Block is something that you are going to create. A My Block is a collection of NXT-G blocks that you have grouped together and may wish to reuse. So let's jump right in and see how this useful feature can help you.

Creating a My Block

Take a look at the following pseudo-code and the matching NXT-G program in Figure 26-1. If SPOT performs these movements, he should follow a square-shaped path and return to his starting position.

Me: SPOT, move forward three rotations and then turn left 90 degrees.

Me: SPOT, move forward another three rotations and then turn left 90 degrees.

Me: SPOT, move forward another three rotations and then turn left 90 degrees.

Me: SPOT, move forward another three rotations and then turn left 90 degrees.

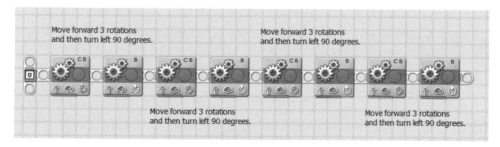

Figure 26-1. *A simple movement program for SPOT*

I could also place the first two MOVE blocks in the program in a LOOP block configured to loop four times, as shown in Figure 26-2.

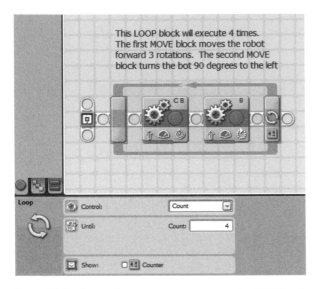

Figure 26-2. *A simple movement program for SPOT using a LOOP block*

But what happens if later I need SPOT to take a Light sensor reading after the second left turn? I would need to modify my two NXT-G programs. The first program (shown in Figure 26-1) isn't that difficult to modify; I just drop in the Light sensor block in the middle of the program, and I'm finished. But for the second program (with the LOOP block), I have to modify the first LOOP block to run twice, then insert the Light sensor block, and finally create a second LOOP block for the final two movements. This is shown in Figure 26-3.

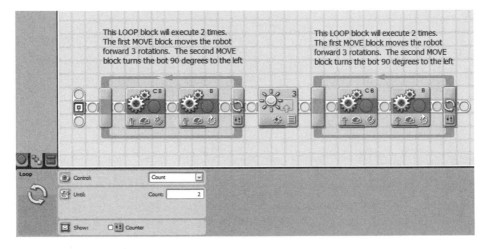

Figure 26-3. *The modified LOOP program*

Now, it wasn't that difficult to modify the program, but imagine if this program is getting larger and larger, with SPOT needing to perform not only left turns but right turns. The program can get quite large with all those MOVE blocks being added. This is where the concept of the My Block comes in handy.

Take a look at Figure 26-4, and then I'll explain what you are seeing.

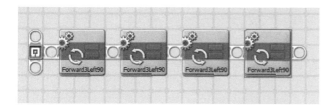

Figure 26-4. *A program using a bunch of My Block blocks*

In Figure 26-4, you'll see four My Block items. Each of these blocks contains two MOVE blocks. The first MOVE block moves the robot forward three rotations, and the second MOVE block turns it left 90 degrees. All I've done is take the program you saw in Figure 26-1 and group the pairs of MOVE blocks. Instead of eight NXT-G blocks (see in Figure 26-1), I now have four My Blocks!

Can you see the value of using My Blocks? Now I have a reusable NXT-G block that I can drop in to this program (or any future program) anytime I want my robot to move forward three rotations and turn left 90 degrees. I could make a similar My Block that moves the robot forward three rotations and turns it right 90 degrees. The options are endless.

By using this concept, I can create collections of NXT-G blocks that perform very specific actions and then bundle them into a My Block and reuse them over and over again. Over time, your My Block collection will grow, and you'll save time by not having to re-create certain actions (such as turn 180 degrees, move forward two rotations, and take a reading on your Light sensor—all three of these actions can be bundled into a single My Block).

So let me show you how you do this.

The first step is to create the repeatable actions you want to bundle in a My Block. To follow my earlier example, I've added two MOVE blocks as shown in Figure 26-5 that will be used to move SPOT forward three rotations and turn him left 90 degrees.

Figure 26-5. *The start of creating a My Block*

After you've created your small NXT-G collection of blocks that you want to make repeatable, click and drag to select the blocks, as shown in Figure 26-6.

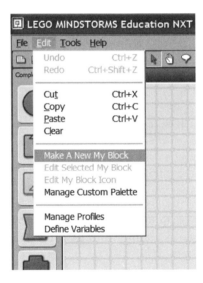

Figure 26-6. *Click and drag to select the blocks you want to include in your My Block.*

Next, click the Edit menu, and select "Make a New My Block" from the available options, as shown in Figure 26-7.

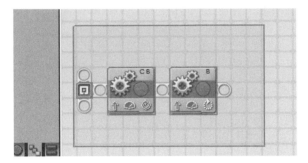

Figure 26-7. *Make a New My Block is selected from the Edit menu.*

The My Block Builder window will appear (see Figure 26-8).

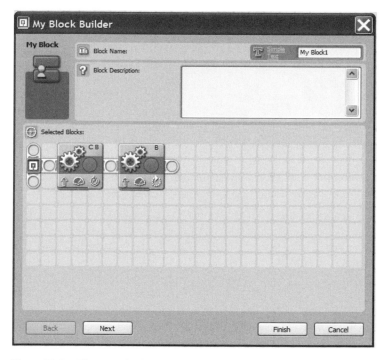

Figure 26-8. *The My Block Builder window*

Fill in the details as shown in Figure 26-9. Give the My Block a name that is useful to you in the Block Name field, and write a more detailed description in the Block Description text box. Click the Next button to choose an icon for your new My Block, or click the Finish button to complete the My Block creation process.

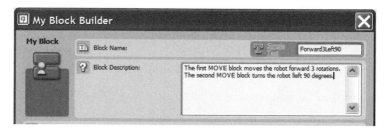

Figure 26-9. *Provide a name and description for your My Block.*

If you click the Next button, you'll see the Icon Builder screen, shown in Figure 26-10. You can drag and drop one or more of the small icons, which are located on the bottom of the window, into the Icon Builder pane. You can see a preview of your new My Block to the right of the Icon Builder workspace.

Figure 26-10. *Create a custom icon for your new My Block.*

Click the Finish button, and that's it. The blocks you selected (in Figure 26-6) are converted to a single My Block that has the name and icon you specified (see Figure 26-11).

Figure 26-11. *Your finished My Block*

You can access your new My Block by clicking the Custom Palette and moving your mouse over the My Blocks palette tool, which is shown in Figure 26-12 (as you can see, I've created quite a few My Blocks, and these appear in the fly-out menu).

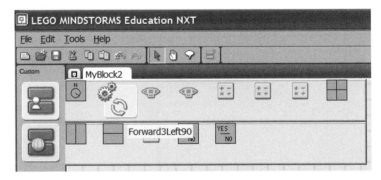

Figure 26-12. *The new My Block appears in the Custom Palette.*

Although it's beyond the scope of this chapter, you should also be aware that My Blocks can receive and send data via data wires. The key to making this work is that the blocks you want to add to a My Block *must* have their data wires configured before you select the blocks and choose "Make a New My Block" from the Edit menu. Any data ports that enter or exit the blocks you have selected will appear as data plugs in your new My Block after you've created it. You'll have to experiment with this ability to determine what will and will not work for you.

Well, that's it! Okay, not exactly. Although I've covered all the NXT-G blocks available in your basic software, this doesn't mean you don't have anything left to learn. As more blocks are created by LEGO and third-party developers, you'll have the ability to add new NXT-G blocks to your palettes, and you'll need to play and experiment with them to learn all the functions and features they provide.

NXT-G is a great way to learn to program robots. Its drag-and-drop interface is easy to use, and you'll find that some very powerful programs can be created with it.

Keep learning, experimenting, and developing new ways to make your robots more responsive, more intelligent, and more impressive. Have fun!

APPENDIX

■ ■ ■

Math Basics for NXT

When programming your robots, you may find many times that you need to perform some basic math in order to properly direct them. While I don't have the space to cover every possible mathematical calculation you may need, I do want to focus on three very simple subjects that you might find useful. The first is converting between degrees and rotations; the second is calculating travel distance based on the number of degrees or rotations you configure; and the third is a very short discussion of how the X/Y coordinate system works on your Brick.

Converting Between Degrees and Rotations

When it comes to the MOVE block's Duration setting on its configuration panel, I've found that most people generally have a preference when configuring their robots to move a specified distance: some will use Degrees, and others will use Rotations. A rare few will rely on Seconds (time-based movement), but if your robot relies at all on accurate movements, you simply cannot program your robot to, say, move forward for 5 seconds and know for a fact that it will move the exact same distance every time (the issue really comes down to batteries—as the batteries become weaker, the motor power is reduced, and those 5 seconds result in a shorter distance than in previous runs).

Whether you prefer degrees or rotations, you may find a time where you need to use the other method; a book or an article might contain a robot you are duplicating, and the MOVE block settings might be in degrees, though you usually work in rotations.

Well, you'll be happy to know that the math for converting back and forth between degrees and rotations is very simple. Take a look at Figure A-1, and I'll give you a couple of examples.

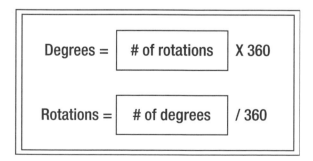

Figure A-1. *Equations for converting between degrees and rotations*

Figure A-1 contains two simple formulas. The top formula is for converting rotations to degrees, and the bottom formula is for converting degrees to rotations. Let me give you an example of each.

Let's say you want SPOT to roll forward 9.5 (nine and a half) rotations—easy enough. But your friend asks you to share your program with her and wants all the MOVE blocks configured in degrees. That's easy enough, too. You simply take a look at Figure A-1 and see that to obtain the value in degrees you need to multiply the number of rotations by 360. Using a calculator or doing it by hand, you'll find that the value in degrees equals 3,420. You go to the configuration panel on the MOVE block, change the Duration setting to Degrees, enter the value of **3420**, and then share your program with your friend.

OK, a week goes by and your friend e-mails you a copy of her version of the program with some modifications. You open the .rbt file and find that she's configured all the MOVE blocks using degrees, but you would really prefer the values to be in rotations. Again, it's easy to change. The bottom formula in Figure A-1 shows that all you need to do is divide the number of degrees by 360. In her first MOVE block, she's configured motor B to spin for 7,543 degrees. If you've done your calculations correctly, you'll find that the value of 7,543 divided by 360 is equal to 20.95277777! Will that work?

Well, the answer is that the MOVE block will only allow you to enter up to three decimal places. It would be safe to enter the value of **20.953** for number of rotations, but you'll find that the NXT motors are really only accurate to the first decimal place. It's your call, and you'll want to experiment with accuracy, but in most cases, you'd be safe entering **20.9** or **21** as the value for rotations. Again, if accuracy is needed, you'll want to do a lot of testing to tweak that value. You might start by using a value of 21 and then reducing it by .1 for each experiment until you get the correct behavior from the motor.

Converting Degrees and Rotations into Distances

OK, you've programmed SPOT to move forward 720 degrees. But how far will that actually move him? What you need is the ability to convert rotations or degrees into inches or centimeters. Well, take a look at Figure A-2, and you'll see some more formulas.

Before I give you an example, remember that to calculate distance you need to convert the Duration value to rotations. So, if your MOVE block has the Duration set in Degrees, use the first formula in Figure A-1 to convert it to rotations.

Now, let me walk you through how to use these simple formulas. In our example, we want to determine how far SPOT will travel if the Duration is set to 720 degrees. We first need to convert that value to rotations, so we simply divide the number of degrees by 360. We end up with 3 rotations.

Next, according to Figure A-2, we need to determine one other value—the wheel circumference. This is easy, and I've given you a small picture to help you. You first measure the diameter of the wheel. The diameter is actually the distance between the two farthest points on the wheel (which happens to be the midpoint of the wheel as well). It doesn't matter if you measure the diameter in inches or centimeters, as long as you remember that the final distance you're going to calculate will also be in those units.

1. Circumference of Wheel = 3.14 × Diameter
2. Distance = Circumference × Rotations

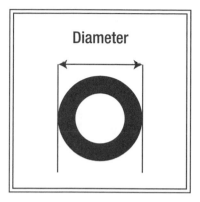

Diameter

Remember to convert Degrees to Rotations before calculating Distance!

Figure A-2. *Calculating distances using rotations or degrees*

If you take one of the NXT wheels and measure it, you'll find that the diameter of the wheel is approximately 2.25 inches (5.715 centimeters). Figure A-2 tells us to find the circumference by multiplying the wheel diameter by 3.14 (also known as pi; pi is a much longer number, but for our calculations, 3.14 is a safe enough approximation). If we've done our math correctly, we obtain a wheel circumference value of 7.065 inches (17.9451 centimeters).

Next, Figure A-2 tells us that we can calculate the total distance moved by multiplying the wheel circumference by the number of rotations. Once again, if we've done our calculations correctly, multiplying 7.065 inches by 3 rotations gives us 21.195 inches (53.8353 centimeters).

And that's it! You can now convert back and forth between rotations and degrees as well as calculate the distances your motors will spin (and that your robots will travel). There's one more small calculation I'll leave you with, but it will involve a quick visit to the Internet.

Would you like to know how to calculate the number of rotations or degrees required to turn your robots left or right? If you want your robot to turn in place without moving forward or backward, how do you calculate the proper number of rotations or degrees to spin one of the motors so that the robot turns left or right?

For the answer (and an example), point your web browser to the following URL:

http://thenxtstep.blogspot.com/2006/10/reader-question-submission-2.html

The X/Y Coordinate System in NXT

The final bit of information I want to provide is how to interpret the coordinate system used on your NXT Brick's LCD screen. The LCD screen has a horizontal resolution of 100 pixels and a vertical resolution of 64 pixels. This simply means you could place 100 small dots across the screen and 64 small dots down the screen. Values actually start with a zero, so the range of coordinates for X are 0–99, and for Y, the range is 0–63.

When using the DISPLAY block (or any block where you must specify a location on the LCD screen), you specify a location by using its horizontal value (X coordinate) and its vertical value (Y coordinate). So, to place a pixel (or dot) directly in the center of the screen, you would have a DISPLAY block place a Point (see Chapter 3 for details on using the DISPLAY block) with an X coordinate of 50 and a Y coordinate of 32.

Some people think there's a trick to using the coordinate system, but it's actually quite simple: coordinates start at 0, 0 in the upper left corner of the LCD screen. Values for X increase as you move to the right, and values for Y increase as you move down the screen. (This is a little different from the X/Y coordinate system you may have learned in school; in that system, X still increases to the right, but Y increases as you move vertically.)

To summarize, the X/Y value of a pixel in the upper-left corner is 0/0. For the upper-right corner, the value would be 99/0. Remember, the Y value only increases as you move down the LCD screen, so the value of a pixel in the lower left corner is 0/63, and a pixel in the lower-right corner is 99/63 (see Figure A-3).

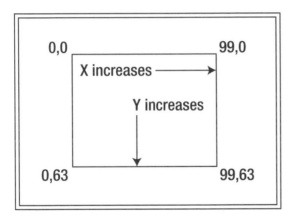

Figure A-3. *The Brick's LCD screen's X/Y Coordinate system*

Index

A

Action data plug, 56
Action section
    CALIBRATE block, 163–164
    FILE ACCESS block, 158
    NXT Rotation sensor, 59
    NXT Touch sensor, 55
    RIS Rotation sensor, 60
    VARIABLE block, 136, 138
Action settings, 34
Addition option, 152
And option, 129
automatic turn-off, 155–156

B

backward movement, 22–23
battery power, 35
Block Description text box, 181
Block Name field, 181
blocks, 8
    CALIBRATE, 163–166
    COMPARE, 105–114
        compared to LOGIC block, 125
        compared to RANGE block, 115
        connection to KEEP ALIVE block, 156
        data plugs, 109
        Equals option, 110
        Greater than option, 110
        Less than option, 110
        Operation section, 109, 127, 129
        preparation for use, 105
    configuration panels, 12
    connecting with data wires, 50
    data hubs, 16–19, 39–46

DISPLAY, 11–16, 102, 111, 153
    Action section, 13, 15
    Display section, 15
    LCD screen, 187
FILE ACCESS, 157–162
    Action section, 158
    data plugs, 161
    Error data plug, 161
    file protection, 158
    File section, 158
    Name section, 158
    rules of use, 157–158
    sequential reading of data, 161
    Type section, 158
    uses, 161
KEEP ALIVE, 155–156
LIGHT SENSOR WAIT, 66
LOGIC, 45, 125–131
    compared to COMPARE block, 125
    testing with SWITCH block, 129
LOOP, 50, 61
    Control section, 75–78
    escapes, 75
    interaction with STOP blocks, 95
    MOVE block inside, 73
    Show section, 75
MATH, 151–153
MOVE, 9, 28
    braking, 27–28
    coasting, 27–28
    configuration panel, 21
    defaults, 22

Duration settings, 25–26, 185
grouping, 179
inside LOOP block, 73
moving backward, 22–23
moving forward, 22–23
Power settings, 25
steering, 24–25
stopping, 24
My Block, 177–183
NUMBER TO TEXT, 101–103
NXT BUTTONS, 60–61
NXT BUTTONS WAIT, 66–67
RANDOM, 99–101, 120
RANGE
compared to COMPARE block, 115
data wires, 120
evaluation by, 115
Operation section, 120
output Result data plug, 121
Slider bar, 120
Test Value data plug, 120
RECEIVE MESSAGE, 173, 175
RECORD/PLAY, 29–32
RESET MOTOR, 167–169
ROTATION SENSOR WAIT, 67
SEND MESSAGE, 171–175
SENSOR, 9, 50
SOUND, 33–37
Action settings, 34
Control settings, 35
Function settings, 35
Note settings, 34
Play option, 35
Stop option, 35
testing, 37
Volume settings, 35
Wait settings, 35–37
SOUND SENSOR WAIT, 67–68
STOP, 95–97
SWITCH, 50, 83–94
Conditions section, 91, 93
Control section, 86
data plug, 90

default condition, 93
Flat view, 85
interaction with STOP blocks, 96
Tabbed view, 85
testing LOGIC block, 129
TEXT, 147–150
TIME WAIT, 14
TIMER, 61
TIMER WAIT, 68
TOUCH SENSOR, 49
TOUCH SENSOR WAIT, 69
ULTRASONIC SENSOR WAIT, 69–70
VARIABLE, 18, 49, 133–145
Action section, 136, 138
configuration with TEXT block, 150
default configuration, 134
example, 141, 144
input data plug, 137
location, 134
memory, 157
Number 1 option, 134
output data plug, 135
Text 1 option, 135
WAIT, 14, 63–70
Control section, 65
LIGHT SENSOR WAIT block, 66
location, 64
NXT BUTTONS WAIT block, 66–67
overview, 63–66
ROTATION SENSOR WAIT block, 67
SOUND SENSOR WAIT block, 67–68
TIMER WAIT block, 68
TOUCH SENSOR WAIT block, 69
ULTRASONIC SENSOR WAIT block, 69–70
Until section, 65
wires, 39–46
Bluetooth connections, 171
braking, 27–28
Brick
buttons, 60
feedback, 53
motor ports, 22

Sleep option, 155
Sleep timer, 155–156
broken wires, 46
buttons, 60–61

C

calculations, 151–153
CALIBRATE block, 163–166
calibration, 163–166
closing data hubs, 17
coasting, 27–28
communication, 171–175
COMPARE block, 105–114
    compared to LOGIC block, 125
    compared to RANGE block, 115
    connection to KEEP ALIVE block, 156
    data plugs, 109
    Operation section, 109–110, 127, 129
    preparation for use, 105
Compare section, 57–60
comparing, 105–114
condition, 53–54
    defined, 72
    sensors, 54
Conditions section, SWITCH block, 91, 93
configuration panels, 12, 167
connecting
    blocks with data wires, 50
    motors, 23
Connection data plugs, 172
Control section
    SWITCH block, 86
    WAIT block, 65
Control settings, 35
controlling wires, 46
conversion
    degrees/rotations, 185–186
    degrees/rotations/distance, 186–188
    pseudo-code, 11
coordinate system, 188

D

data hubs
    closing, 17
    defined, 17

expanding, 49
NXT Touch sensor, 55
opening, 17
viewing, 42
data plugs
    COMPARE block, 109
    FILE ACCESS block, 161
    input plugs, 18, 43
    NUMBER TO TEXT block, 103
    output plugs, 18, 43
    SWITCH block, 90
    viewing names, 46
    Yes/No Logic plug, 49
data storage, 157–162
data wires
    My Block, 182
    RANGE block, 120
    RECEIVE MESSAGE block, 175
    SEND MESSAGE block, 172, 175
default conditions, SWITCH block, 93
Define Variables menu option, 139
degrees
    conversion to distance, 186–188
    conversion to/from rotations, 185–186
Degrees option, 26
DISPLAY block, 11–16, 102, 111, 153
    Action section, 13–16
    LCD screen, 188
displaying random numbers, 101–103
distance, conversion from degrees/rotations, 186–188
Division option, 152
Drawing option, 16
Drawing tool, 16
Duration settings, 22, 25–26

E

Edit menu, "Make a New My Block" option, 180
Equals option, COMPARE block, 110
"error correction" activity, shutting off, 168
Error data plug, 161
escapes, 75
executing programs, 3

∎F

feedback, 53–62
    Brick, 53
    buttons, 54
    condition, 53–54
    motors, 53
    NXT buttons, 60–61
    NXT timers, 60–61
    sensors, 53–60
        NXT Light sensor, 57–58
        NXT Rotation sensor, 59
        NXT Sound sensor, 57
        NXT Touch sensor, 55–56
        NXT Ultrasonic sensor, 58–59
        overview, 54–55
        RIS Light sensor, 58
        RIS Rotation sensor, 59–60
        RIS Temperature sensor, 60
        RIS Touch sensor, 56–57
    timers, 54
FILE ACCESS block, 157–162
    Action section, 158
    data plugs, 161
    Error data plug, 161
    file protection, 158
    File section, 158
    Name section, 158
    rules of use, 157–158
    sequential reading of data, 161
    Type section, 158
    uses, 161
File section, FILE ACCESS block, 158
Flat view, SWITCH block, 85
forward movement, 22–23
Function settings, 35

∎G

Generate light box, NXT Light sensor, 58
generating random numbers, 99–101
Greater than option, COMPARE block, 110

∎H

Help menu, 56

∎I

icons, choosing for My Block, 181
Image option, 15
information sharing, 171–175
information storage, 133–145
input data, 41
input plugs, 18, 43
    MATH block, 152
    VARIABLE block, 137
Inside Range option, RANGE block, 120
installing NXT-G programming software, 5
integers, 151

∎K

KEEP ALIVE block, 155–156
keyboards, 43–44

∎L

LCD screen resolution, 188
leading spaces, 148
Less than option, COMPARE block, 110
lifting, 25
LIGHT SENSOR WAIT block, 66
light sensors, 178
    calibration, 163–165
    NXT, 57–58
    RIS, 58
LOGIC block, 125–131
    compared to COMPARE block, 125
    testing with SWITCH block, 129
Logic blocks, 45
Logic data, 46, 133
logic keyboards, 44
logical responses, 47–51
LOOP block, 50, 61, 73
    Control section
        Count option, 77
        Forever option, 76
        Logic option, 78
        Sensor section, 76
        Time option, 75
    escapes, 75

interaction with STOP blocks, 95
MOVE block inside, 73
Show section, 75
loop breaks, 75
looping, defined, 73

M

Mailbox section
RECEIVE MESSAGE block, 173
SEND MESSAGE block, 172
mailboxes, 172
maintaining activity, 155–156
"Make a New My Block" option, 180
MATH block, 151–153
memory, 157–162
Message section, RECEIVE MESSAGE block, 173
motors
connecting, 23
Duration, 22
feedback, 53
pairing, 167
ports, 22
Power, 22
resetting, 167–169
spin direction, 22
MOVE block, 9, 21–28
braking, 27–28
coasting, 27–28
configuration panel, 21–22
defaults, 22
Duration setting, 185
Duration settings, 25–26
grouping, 179
inside LOOP block, 73
moving backward, 22–23
moving forward, 22–23
Power settings, 25
steering, 24–25
stopping, 24
movements
backward, 22–23
forward, 22–23
naming, 30

playing back, 29–32
precision, 168
recording, 29–32
repetition of, 71–78
spinning, 25
square-shaped path, 71, 177
time-based, 185
timing, 31
Multiplication option, MATH block, 152
My Block, 177–183
accessing, 182
Block Description text box, 181
Block Name field, 181
choosing icon for, 181
creating, 177–183
data wires, 182

N

Name section, FILE ACCESS block, 158
naming recorded movements, 30
nested loops, 78–81
Not option, COMPARE block, 129
Note settings, 34
number data, 46, 133
NUMBER TO TEXT block, 101–103
NXT buttons, 60–61
NXT BUTTONS block, 60–61
NXT BUTTONS WAIT block, 66–67
NXT-G programming software, 4–6
NXT Light sensor, 57–58
NXT Rotation sensor, 59
NXT Sound sensor, 57
NXT timers, 60–61
NXT Touch sensor, 55–56
NXT Ultrasonic sensor, 58–59

O

opening data hubs, 17
Operation section
COMPARE block, 109, 127
MATH block, 152
RANGE block, 120
Or option, COMPARE block, 129
output data, 41

Find it faster at http://superindex.apress.com

output plugs, 18, 43
  MATH block, 152
  RANDOM block, 120
  VARIABLE block, 135
Outside Range option, RANGE block, 120

■P
paths, defined, 84
Play option, 32, 35
playing back movements, 29–32
Port data plug, NXT Touch sensor, 56
Port section, CALIBRATE block, 163
ports
  NXT Light sensor, 57
  NXT Rotation sensor, 59
  NXT Sound sensor, 57
  NXT Touch sensor, 55
  NXT Ultrasonic sensor, 58
  RIS Light sensor, 58
  RIS Rotation sensor, 59
  RIS Temperature sensor, 60
  RIS Touch sensor, 57
Power settings, 22, 25
prerecorded sounds, 34
Pressed option, 49
program structure, 7–9
programming
  defined, 1–4
  logic, 105
  logical responses, 47–51
  nested loops, 78–81
  NXT-G, 4–6
  overview, 1
  playing back movements, 29–32
  recording movements, 29–32
  robots, 1
  specificity, 4, 7
  structure, 7–9
programs, executing and running, 3
pseudo-code, 7–8, 11
pushing, 25

■R
RANDOM block, 99–101
  output Number data plug, 120
  Range section, 100

random numbers, 99–103
  displaying, 101–103
  generating, 99–101
RANGE block, 115–123
  compared to COMPARE block, 115
  data wires, 120
  evaluation by, 115
  Operation section, 120
  output Result data plug, 121
  Slider bar, 120
  Test Value data plug, 120
Range section, RANDOM block, 100
Raw Value data plug, 56
RECEIVE MESSAGE block, 173, 175
Record option, 30
RECORD/PLAY block, 29–32
  location, 30
  Play option, 32
  Record option, 30
recording movements, 29–32
remote controls, 175
repetition of movements, 71–78
RESET MOTOR block, 167–169
Reset option, 16
resetting motors, 167–169
Result data plug, 152
RIS. See Robotics Invention System
Robo Center, 5
Robo Educator, 5
Robotics Invention System (RIS)
  compatibility with NXT, 54
  Light sensor, 58
  Rotation sensor, 59–60
  Temperature sensor, 60
  Touch sensor, 56–57
robots overview, 1–6
ROTATION SENSOR WAIT block, 67
rotation sensors
  NXT, 59
  RIS, 59–60
rotations
  conversion to distance, 186–187
  conversion to/from degrees, 185–186
Rotations option, 26
running programs, 3

S

screens, 43

Seconds option, 26

SEND MESSAGE block, 171–175

sensor blocks, 9, 50

Sensor option, SWITCH block, 86

Sensor section, CALIBRATE block, 163

sensors, 54–60

    condition, 54

    feedback, 53

    NXT Light, 57–58

    NXT Rotation, 59

    NXT Sound, 57

    NXT Touch, 55–56

    NXT Ultrasonic, 58–59

    overview, 54–55

    RIS Light, 58

    RIS Rotation, 59–60

    RIS Temperature, 60

    RIS Touch, 56–57

setting minimum/maximum values, 163–166

sharing information, 171–175

Show section

    NXT Ultrasonic sensor, 59

    RIS Temperature sensor, 60

Sleep option, 155

Sleep timer, 155–156

Slider bar, 120

SOUND block, 33–37

    Action settings, 34

    Control settings, 35

    Function settings, 35

    Note settings, 34

    Play option, 35

    Stop option, 35

    testing, 37

    Volume settings, 35

    Wait for Completion checkbox, 36–37

    Wait settings, 35–37

Sound File option, 34

SOUND SENSOR WAIT block, 67–68

sound sensors, 57, 163, 165

sounds, 33–37

    battery power, 35

    overview, 33

    prerecorded, 34

    selecting notes, 34

    SOUND block, 33–37

        Action settings, 34

        Control settings, 35

        Function settings, 35

        Note settings, 34

        Volume settings, 35

        Wait settings, 35–37

    timing, 34

spinning, 25

steering, 24–25

STOP block, 95–97

    data hub, 95

    interaction with LOOP blocks, 95

    interaction with SWITCH blocks, 96

    testing tool, 96

Stop option, SOUND block, 35

stopping, 24

storage of information, 133–145

strings, 148

Subtraction option, MATH block, 152

surface conditions, 25

SWITCH block, 50, 83–94

    Conditions section, 91, 93

    Control section, 86

    data plug, 90

    default condition, 93

    Flat view, 85

    interaction with STOP blocks, 96

    Tabbed view, 85

    testing LOGIC block, 129

T

Tabbed view, SWITCH block, 85

temperature sensors, RIS, 60

Test Value data plug, 120

testing use of SOUND blocks, 37

TEXT block, 147–150

text data, 46

Find it faster at http://superindex.apress.com

Text data plugs, 148
Text option, 16
TIME WAIT block, 14
TIMER block, 61
TIMER WAIT block, 68
timers, 60–61
    feedback, 54
    TIMER WAIT block, 68
timing
    recorded movements, 31
    sounds, 34
Tone option, 34
TOUCH SENSOR block, 49
TOUCH SENSOR WAIT block, 69
touch sensors
    NXT, 55–56
    RIS, 56–57
true/false responses, 125–131
Type section, FILE ACCESS block, 158

■U
ULTRASONIC SENSOR WAIT block, 69–70
ultrasonic sensors, NXT, 58–59
Unlimited option, 26
Until section, WAIT block, 65

■V
Value option, SWITCH block, 89
Value section, CALIBRATE block, 164
values, testing whether falls inside or outside
        of numbers, 115–123
VARIABLE block, 18, 49, 133–145
    Action section, 136, 138
    configuration with TEXT block, 150
    default configuration, 134
    example, 141, 144
    input data plug, 137
    location, 134
    memory, 157
    Number 1 option, 134
    output data plug, 135
    Text 1 option, 135
variables, 133, 139
Volume settings, 35

■W
WAIT block, 14, 63–70
    Control section, 65
    LIGHT SENSOR WAIT block, 66
    location, 64
    NXT BUTTONS WAIT block, 66–67
    overview, 63–66
    ROTATION SENSOR WAIT block, 67
    SOUND SENSOR WAIT block, 67–68
    TIMER WAIT block, 68
    TOUCH SENSOR WAIT block, 69
    ULTRASONIC SENSOR WAIT block, 69–70
    Until section, 65
Wait for Completion checkbox, SOUND
        block, 36–37
Wait settings, 35–37
wheel circumference, 186
wires, 39–46, 50
words, 147–150
Write option, VARIABLE block, 136

■X
X/Y coordinate system, 187
Xor option, COMPARE block, 129

■Y
yes/no answers, 47–51, 125–131
Yes/No data plug, 56

You Need the Companion eBook

Your purchase of this book entitles you to buy the companion PDF-version eBook for only $10. Take the weightless companion with you anywhere.

We believe this Apress title will prove so indispensable that you'll want to carry it with you everywhere, which is why we are offering the companion eBook (in PDF format) for $10 to customers who purchase this book now. Convenient and fully searchable, the PDF version of any content-rich, page-heavy Apress book makes a valuable addition to your programming library. You can easily find and copy code—or perform examples by quickly toggling between instructions and the application. Even simultaneously tackling a donut, diet soda, and complex code becomes simplified with hands-free eBooks!

Once you purchase your book, getting the $10 companion eBook is simple:

❶ Visit **www.apress.com/promo/tendollars/**.

❷ Complete a basic registration form to receive a randomly generated question about this title.

❸ Answer the question correctly in 60 seconds, and you will receive a promotional code to redeem for the $10.00 eBook.

eBookshop

2855 TELEGRAPH AVENUE | SUITE 600 | BERKELEY, CA 94705

Offer valid through 1/16/08.